Thomas Cook

HOTSPOTS
CORFU

Written by Kerry Fisher; updated by Jeroen van Marle

Published by Thomas Cook Publishing
A division of Thomas Cook Tour Operations Limited.
Company registration no. 1450464 England
The Thomas Cook Business Park, Unit 9, Coningsby Road,
Peterborough PE3 8SB, United Kingdom
Email: sales@thomascook.com, Tel: + 44 (0)1733 416477
www.thomascookpublishing.com

Produced by Cambridge Publishing Management Limited
Burr Elm Court, Main Street, Caldecote CB23 7NU

ISBN: 978-1-84157-890-3

First edition © 2006 Thomas Cook Publishing
This second edition © 2008
Text © Thomas Cook Publishing,
Maps © Thomas Cook Publishing/PCGraphics (UK) Limited

Series Editor: Diane Ashmore
Production/DTP: Steven Collins

Printed and bound in Spain by GraphyCems

Cover photography © Thomas Cook

CONTENTS

INTRODUCTION 5
Getting to know Corfu 8
The best of Corfu 10
Symbols key 12

RESORTS 13
Corfu Town 15
Perama 20
Moraitika & Messonghi 24
Kavos 27
Aghios Georgios (south-west)..30
Aghios Gordios 33
Glyfada & Pelekas 36
Ermones 39
Paleokastritsa 43
Aghios Georgios (north-west)...47
Arillas 49
Aghios Stefanos 51
Sidari 55
Roda 60
Acharavi 63
Kassiopi 66
Kalami 68
Nissaki 70
Barbati 72
Ipsos 74
Dassia 79
Kontokali & Gouvia 81

EXCURSIONS 85
Achilleion Palace 86
Albania 88
Parga 91
Paxos 93

LIFESTYLE 95
Food & drink 96
Menu decoder 100
Shopping 102
Children 104
Sports & activities 106
Festivals & events 109

PRACTICAL INFORMATION ..111
Accommodation 112
Preparing to go 114
During your stay 118

INDEX 125

MAPS
Corfu 6
Corfu Town 14
Paleokastritsa 42
Sidari 54
Paxos, Antipaxos
   & Parga 90

WHAT'S IN YOUR GUIDEBOOK?

Independent authors Impartial, up-to-date information from our travel experts who meticulously source local knowledge.

Experience Thomas Cook's 165 years in the travel industry and guidebook publishing enriches every word with expertise you can trust.

Travel know-how Contributions by thousands of staff around the globe, each one living and breathing travel.

Editors Travel-publishing professionals, pulling everything together to craft a perfect blend of words, pictures, maps and design.

You, the traveller We deliver a practical, no-nonsense approach to information, geared to how you really use it.

● *Sunset in Arillas*

INTRODUCTION
Getting to know Corfu

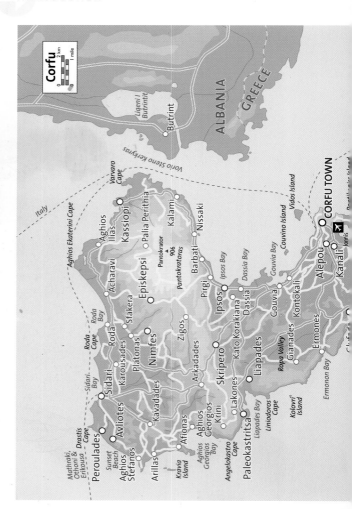

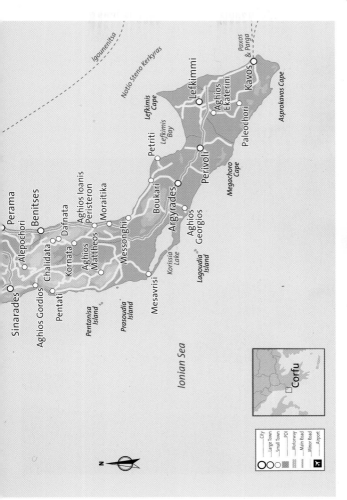

Getting to know Corfu

Corfu is the northernmost of the Ionian islands and the second largest in the group. It lies just off the west coast of the Greek mainland and only a few kilometres (a couple of miles) from Albania. In the shape of a sickle, it is about 64 km (40 miles) long and 29 km (18 miles) across. Despite its relatively small size, this olive-tree-covered island encompasses a variety of vegetation, architecture and activities to delight and fascinate visitors.

● *Sidari coastline*

Corfu is known as 'Kerkyra' in Greek. Legend has it that the name comes from a nymph called Korkyra, who was brought to the island by her lover, Poseidon, the god of the sea. In ancient Greek literature, Homer refers to Corfu as the home of the Phaeacians, also calling it Scheria. In the Odyssey, he mentions the island when recounting the story of Odysseus who was shipwrecked on his way home to Ithaca. He was washed up on a beach before being rescued by the beautiful Princess Nausicaa. Paleokastritsa is the top contender for the beach in question, although several others, like Ermones, also stake a claim.

HISTORICAL CORFU

Although the island has adapted to accommodate the tourist market, with full English breakfasts, pizza and trendy brands of beer, Corfu remains essentially Greek, with a delightful combination of other cultural influences. Its position between Greece and Italy made it a sought-after maritime stronghold, occupied by various nations over the centuries, and the architecture on the island today is a legacy of its chequered past. Nowhere is this more obvious than in Corfu Town, where elegant Venetian houses line a labyrinth of narrow alleys and the arcaded French-built Liston stands metres from the imposing British palace of SS Michael and George.

BEACHES, RESORTS AND NATURE

The vast majority of visitors comes for the sun, sea and sand, and with its reliably warm weather, crystal-clear water and miles of Blue Flag sand and shingle beaches, Corfu won't disappoint. Apart from Corfu Town, there are several large purpose-built resorts that offer everything from watersports to a vibrant nightlife. However, the charm of Corfu lies in the smaller, less developed seaside fishing villages with just a handful of tavernas, and these peaceful havens are well worth seeking out. Nature lovers can head inland, where countless walking and horse riding paths criss-cross the island, linking quiet rural villages with the mountains and forests of central Corfu.

THE BEST OF CORFU

On Corfu there are golden sands to relax and sunbathe on, plenty of watersports centres offering everything from water-skiing to scuba diving, excellent local cuisine, and the shopping is good, too! Here's a short overview of the best of Corfu:

- **Sunbathe** on the quiet, sandy expanse at **Aghios Georgios** (south-west, see page 30) or on Corfu's most beautifully situated beach at **Aghios Gordios** (see page 33).

- **Wander around historical Corfu Town** and visit one of the imposing fortresses, candle-lit churches and excellent museums (see page 15).

- **Visit the Achilleion Palace** (see page 86) for the over-the-top decoration, beautiful gardens and the Dying Achilles statue.

- **Spend a morning shopping** for souvenirs in Corfu Town's lively shopping area (see page 19).

- **Explore life below the waves** with a scuba diving trip, for instance in Paleokastritsa (see page 43) or Aghios Georgios (north-west, see page 47).

- **Climb up to Theotokos Monastery** (see page 45) with its peaceful atmosphere, lovely terraces and views.

- **Venture into nature** along the flower-scented path up to the chapel at Aghios Stefanos (see page 52).

- **Energetic holidaymakers** will never forget the hike up to the peak of **Mount Pantokrator** (see pages 63 & 75), the ultimate on-top-of-the-world sensation.

- **Explore** the evocative ancient ruins at **Butrint** on a day trip to **Albania** (see page 88).

- **Party** the night away in **Kavos** (see page 27), Corfu's number one youth resort.

◆ *View across to Albania from Mount Pantokrator*

SYMBOLS KEY

The following symbols are used throughout this book:

ⓐ address ☏ telephone ⓦ website address ⓔ email
🕒 opening times ⓘ important

The following symbols are used on the maps:

𝑖	information office	◯	city
✉	post office	◯	large town
🏢	shopping	◌	small town
✈	airport	▦	POI (point of interest)
✚	hospital	═	motorway
🛡	police station	━	main road
🚌	bus station	—	minor road
✝	church		

❶ numbers denote featured cafés, restaurants & evening venues

RESTAURANT CATEGORIES

Restaurant price ratings (average main course plus starter/
dessert and drink):

£ = under €12   ££ = between €12 and €25   £££ = over €25

▶ *Corfu's miles of sandy beaches cannot fail to please*

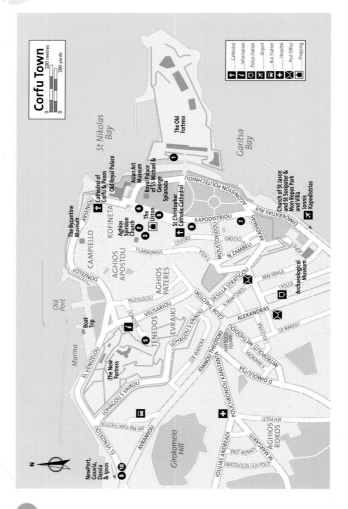

Corfu Town

0 ___ 200 metres
0 ___ 200 yards

Cathedral
Information
Police Station
Airport
Bus Station
Hospital
Post Office
Shopping

St Nikolas Bay

Garitsa Bay

The Old Fortress ❶

ANAGNOSTON POUTCHNIOU

Cathedral of Corfu & Paxos
Old Royal Palace
Asian Art Museum
Royal Palace of SS Michael & George
Spianada

ARSENIOU

KOFINETA

The Byzantine Museum

CAMPIELLO

Aghios Spiridon Church ❸

The Liston ❹

St Christopher Catholic Cathedral ❻

KAPODISTRIOU

❾

❼

DIMOKRATIAS AVE

Church of St Jason and St Sosipater & Mon Repos Park and Villa

Ioannis Kapodistrias

AGHIOS APOSTOLI

FILARMONIKIS

MOUSTOXIDOU

GYLFORD

N ZAMBELI

D IOLA

GYLFORD

DONZELOT

AGHIOS PATERES

PALEOLOGOU

GEOR THEOTOKI

DESILLA STRATGOU

N MANTZAROU

I POLILA

ARM VRAILA

Archaeological Museum

ALEXANDRAS

KSIRIOU

Old Port

VELISARIOU

EVRAIKI

LOHAGOU S VAIKOU

IOANNOU THEOTOKI

Boat Trip

TENEDOS ❺

❷

LOHAGOU S VAIKOU

SAN ROCCO SQUARE

GR MARKORA

MITROPOLITI METHODIOU

GR MARASLI

Marina

EL VENIZELOU

The New Fortress

LOHAGOU S VAIKOU

9th PAR IOAN THEOTOKI

POLCHRONIOU KANSTANTA

D DIMOULITSA

AGHIOS ROKOS

M MAKARITI

N ___

New Port, Gouvia, Dassia & Ipsos

EL VENIZELOU

AVRAMIOU

Girokomeio Hill

IOULIAS ANDREADI

EROT MORAITI

EMATOLOGOU ILIA POLITI

ATH POLTI

❽ ❿

❿

Corfu Town

Every narrow alley or arcaded street in the island's capital offers up a host of entrancing images. The Venetians ruled Corfu from 1386 to 1797 and the architecture has a strong Italian influence, with little squares and ornate wells nestling below elegant churches and bell towers.

THINGS TO SEE & DO

Aghios Spiridon Church

This red-domed church is dedicated to the shepherd-turned-bishop who is credited with saving the island from many disasters, not least the Turkish siege in 1716. His remains, smuggled on a donkey from Constantinople to Corfu in the 15th century, are in a silver reliquary to the right of the altar.

ⓐ One block behind the Liston in Aghios Spiridon Square
ⓣ 26610 33059 ⓛ 09.00–14.00 ⓘ Donations welcome

Archaeological Museum

Great for visiting on hot afternoons due to the cool air-conditioning, this small museum contains a wealth of finds, including finds from the Mon Repos estate, a 6th-century BC stone lion and the magnificent Gorgon Pediment, the frieze of the Doric Temple of Artemis.

ⓐ 5 Armeni Vraila ⓣ 26610 30680 ⓛ 08.30–15.00 Tues–Sun
ⓘ Admission charge

Asian Art Museum

A unique collection of Asian art, donated to the state by a former diplomat in 1927 and expanded ever since. There are statues, paintings and objects from China, Japan, India, Tibet, Cambodia and other countries. The beautiful British-built palace from 1824 is worth the entrance fee alone.

ⓐ Royal Palace of SS Michael and George ⓣ 26610 30443
ⓛ 08.00–19.30 Tues–Sun ⓘ Admission charge

The Byzantine Museum

The restored church of Antivouniotissa houses a collection of religious
artefacts, majestic silver candelabra and 15th- to 19th-century icons.
It has a beautiful garden at the back, complete with bell tower.

ⓐ In the Church of Antivouniotissa, off Arseniou Street, up the steps
ⓘ 26610 38313 ⓒ 08.30–14.30 Tues–Sun, closed Mon ⓘ Admission charge

Church of St Jason and St Sosipater

Walking back from Mon Repos to Corfu Town, a left turn before the
Marina Hotel leads you to the 10th- to 11th-century octagonal-domed
Byzantine church, dedicated to two of St Paul's disciples, credited with
bringing Christianity to Corfu around AD 48.

ⓒ 08.00–19.00

The Liston

The Liston is an arcaded promenade built in 1807 on the instructions
of Napoleon as an imitation of the Parisian Rue de Rivoli. Its name is
derived from the Venetian *libro d'oro*, an exclusive golden book listing
the names of the aristocrats who were allowed to walk here. It still has
a stylish air about it, and is filled with cafés and restaurants.

Mon Repos Park and Villa

The access to this pretty wooded park is through green iron gates,
opposite the ruined Palaiopolis basilica. It was built for the British High
Commissioner, Frederic Adam, in 1824 and later served as a summer
residence for the Greek royal family. Prince Philip, Duke of Edinburgh,
was born here in 1921. The restored villa is open to the public as the very
enjoyable Palaiopolis Museum.

ⓒ Grounds open 08.00–19.00; museum 08.30–15.00 Tues–Sun
ⓘ Grounds free; admission charge for museum

The New Fortress

Overlooking the marina in the old town, the new fortress was built by
the Venetians in 1576 to strengthen the town's defences after one of

many attacks by the Turks. You can climb to the top for views over the town and across the sea to Albania. There is also a cool, stone café with arrow slits for windows. ⓐ The entrance is just after the Tenedos church in Solomos Street 🕓 09.00–20.30 ❗ Small admission charge

The Old Fortress

Defences were constructed on the twin peaks of the fortress as early as the 6th century. Most of the fortifications there today were built by the Venetians in the 15th and 16th centuries. Climb up to the top for wonderful views.

ⓐ Spianada 🕓 08.30–19.30 Tues–Sun ❗ Admission charge

Boat trip

Book a trip on the *Kalypso Star* and experience the wonderful world beneath the sea through bay windows. There's also an excellent underwater show with sea lions and a diver.

ⓐ Old Port ☎ 26610 46525 🕓 Hourly 10.00–18.00, Sun 11.00–16.00

🔺 *The red dome of Aghios Spiridon church rises high over Corfu Town*

TAKING A BREAK

Art Café £ ❶ Corfu Town's most pleasant café, in the sheltered gardens behind the Palace of SS Michael and George. Sit beneath palm trees, enjoy great sea views and have coffee, drinks or light snacks. ⓐ Spianada ☎ 26610 49366 ⏰ 09.00–02.00

Biocafé £ ❷ Proving that organic food can be tasty as well as affordable, the fantastic Biocafé serves a delicious full meal for under €8, using only local, pesticide-free products. There's also organic crêpes, fruit juices, ice cream and even organic beer. ⓐ 15 Iroon Square ☎ 26610 37761 ⏰ 07.30–01.00

Mikro Café £ ❸ A tiny café in the heart of town where you can have a coffee along the street or in a small garden terrace. ⓐ 42 Kotardou, corner N. Theotoki ☎ 22610 31009 ⏰ 09.30–02.00, 19.00–02.00 Sun

Café au Chocolat ££ ❹ On the northern corner of the Liston, this modern café is great place to chill with ice cream, cocktails and smoothies. ⓐ Eleftherieas Square ☎ 26610 80019 ⏰ 09.00–02.00

Stablus ££–£££ ❺ The glitziest bar and restaurant in town, set beautifully beside a small church and beneath the walls of the New Fortress. There's excellent Mediterranean cuisine, a designer bar and a very pleasant garden. ⓐ 29 Solomou ☎ 26610 35720 ⏰ 11.00–16.00 and 20.00–01.00, 11.00–01.00 Sun.

Aegli £££ ❻ The perfect place for watching chic Corfiots sashay by. Serves a mixture of Greek specialities and innovative cuisine. ⓐ 23 Kapodistriou Street, Liston ☎ 26610 31949 ⏰ 09.00–24.00

Cavalieri Roof Garden £££ ❼ A fantastic rooftop restaurant with quality Greek and international food, but you can also just come for coffee or cocktails from the bar. Be sure to book ahead for the best tables. ⓐ 4 Kapodistriou ❶ 26610 39041 ❶ 10.00–02.00

AFTER DARK

There are plenty of bars in town, but for serious and loud clubbing, most people head to the famed disco strip along Ethnikis Antistaseos, a few kilometres out of town towards Dassia.

Au Bar ❽ Corfu's best and most happening club, with a beautiful garden area. A popular venue for big-name foreign DJs. ⓐ 30 Antistaseos, disco strip ❶ 26610 80909 ❶ 22.00–06.00

Gala Café ❾ A nicely designed cocktail bar in the middle of the club strip. A good place to catch your breath between clubs. ⓐ 40 Ethnikis Antistaseos, disco strip ❶ 26610 40701 ❶ 09.00–03.00

EY Café ££ ❿ A trendy modern lounge café overlooking the park, and serving international fusion cuisine, great coffee, wine and cocktails. Regular parties and free wifi too. ⓐ 32 Kapodistriou ❶ 26610 80670 ❶ 09.00–03.00

SHOPPING

Shoppers will find all the olive wood, jewellery and clothes they can carry west of the Spianada, and on picturesque, arcaded Nikiforou Theotoki Street. In early morning, head to the fruit and vegetable market in the moat of the new fortress for a slice of true Corfiot life.
Koriem Ceramics. Handmade Corfiot-style ceramic plates and masks with flower patterns. ⓐ 56 Guilford ❶ 26610 45610 ❶ 09.00–13.00 and 15.30–22.00 Mon–Fri
Rosie's Bakery Traditional sweets made without eggs or butter which will last up to 15 days, making unusal treats.
ⓐ 71 Palaiologou ❶ 02915 6573 ❶ 09.00–12.00 & 15.00–21.00

Perama

Situated halfway between the island's capital and the lively seaside
village of **Benitses** (see below), Perama lies on the steep shoreline south
of Corfu Town amongst lush green vegetation. Plane spotters will love
the sight of aircraft cruising in to land at close range.

BEACHES

Perama has a pleasant shingle beach reached by steep steps leading
down from the main road. The shingle beach at Benitses is south of the
old village alongside the main road and has a good range of watersports
on offer. Aghios Ioannis, 4 km (2¹/₂ miles) south, also has good
watersports from its sandy beach.

THINGS TO SEE & DO

Aghios Ioannis (St John's)

Just south of Benitses is the small resort of Aghios Ioannis (St John's),
with its narrow but clean and sandy beach and plenty of water
activities on offer, including boat trips. The Melia Marbella Hotel
beach is furthest from the busy road running immediately beside
the beach, and can be accessed along a path beside the tunnel.
There are some good tavernas with beachside terraces, including
the Marbella Fish Taverna (**££** ❶ 26610 72268 ❷ 10.00–01.00) along the
main road just before the tunnel. The La Terrazza (**££–£££**) restaurant
at the Melia Marbella has superb views across the sea and towards
Corfu Town. There is a regular green bus service to Corfu Town – a trip
of about 45–60 minutes.

Benitses

A stroll through the old village is like venturing into a secret garden
through a pretty maze of narrow alleys, lemon orchards and
whitewashed houses. This is reputedly the home of the oldest olive tree

in Greece – an amazing 750 years old. Benitses' seafront is a mass of bars and tavernas, just right for a lively evening out. The **Corfu Shell Museum** in Benitses is one of Europe's largest shell collections. The highlights include a cowrie shell from Mozambique, listed in the *Guinness World Records* as the most precious shell in the world. Exotic souvenirs and unusual shells for collectors are on sale.

ⓐ North end of Benitses Harbour Square ① 26610 72227 ① 09.30–20.00
① Admission charge

🔻 *Vlacherena Monastery with Pontikonisi (Mouse Island) behind*

> ## MOUSE ISLAND?
> There are several theories as to why Pontikonisi is called Mouse Island, including that it was once home to a million of the creatures, that it refers to its shape, or that it is just mouse size – it's for you to decide!

Kanoni peninsula

The Kanoni peninsula, a short walk across the pedestrian causeway separating Halkiopolous Lagoon from the sea and also easily reached from Corfu Town makes for a great trip. You can walk along the causeway (directly below the flight path of incoming planes) past the picturesque little **Vlacherena Monastery** and the harbour to the winding steps leading up the hill. The famous view from here over **Pontikonisi (Mouse Island)** and the monastery is stunning. Take a boat to Pontikonisi from Perama to the monastery and admire the Byzantine chapel hidden beneath the cypress trees. Further up the hill you can visit **Analipsis**, whose spring used to supply fresh water to Venetian ships. The spring is now a trickle and the inscription says those who drink from it will never see their homeland again! Carry on down the path to a tiny cove for a dip. The largest part of the top of Analipsis hill is dominated by the **Mon Repos estate** (page 16).

TAKING A BREAK

Captain's Taverna £ 'Captain' George's patter continues while he cooks and serves homemade Greek food at its best. Little touches such as grilled pitta bread with your *taramasalata* and *tzatziki* are most welcome, but leave room for your main course. The portions are very generous – gargantuan meals at less than gargantuan prices. A favourite for everyone and there's a safe playground for children too. ⓐ Just after the viewpoint, Kanoni ⓣ 26610 40502 ⓛ 09.00–23.00

Pontikonisi Café £ A breezy café off the main road, with excellent views of the beach, sea and islands below. Guests can use the small hotel pool to cool down. ⓐ Main road ⓣ 69477 48818 ⓛ 09.00–01.00

Nausicaa ££ Excellent, very popular restaurant serving Greek and international dishes and delicious puddings, from chocolate mousse to Greek *baklavas*. ⓐ 11 Nafsikas, Kanoni, opposite Divani Hotel ⓣ 26610 23492 ⓛ 17.00–24.00

Taverna S Sofia ££ Live music accompanies friendly service at this upmarket Italian restaurant and piano bar with a large terrace overlooking the sea. If you've overdosed on *retsina*, rich red Italian wines flow freely here. ⓐ Northern side of the main street ⓣ 26610 21145 ⓛ 11.30–23.00

Alkinoos £££ Enjoy some of the best views in Perama from the terraces of this classy restaurant. The chicken is chargrilled to perfection and delicious Roquefort, wine or mushroom sauces complement the succulent steaks. ⓐ On the north side of the main road, opposite Avra Pub ⓣ 26610 41848 ⓛ 10.00–23.00

AFTER DARK

If you're feeling lucky, spend an evening at the casino in the **Corfu Holiday Palace Hotel**. ⓐ 2 Nafsikas, Kanoni ⓣ 26610 46941 ⓦ www.corfuholidaypalace.gr ⓛ 20.00–03.00 ❶ There's a strict dress code, and don't forget your passport!

Moraitika & Messonghi

Moraitika and Messonghi share the same long sweep of fine grey sand and shingle beach. Moraitika is larger and livelier, with plenty of restaurants and bars along the coastal road leading south to Messonghi. For a peaceful lunchtime or romantic evening, the old village up on the hillside has a couple of traditional tavernas in the maze of cobbled streets and whitewashed, flower-hung houses.

THINGS TO SEE & DO

Boat trip
Messonghi Cruises run trips to Corfu Town, around the north-east coast and to the Blue Lagoon. A man called Zorba runs trips to southern Corfu – find him on his boat at the mouth of the river between 17.30 and 21.30.

Boukari
A short bike ride along the quiet coastal road south of Messonghi you'll pass the fishing hamlet of Boukari, where there are several excellent fresh fish tavernas, quiet beaches and forests coming down from the hills to the waterfront.

Tennis
Have a game of tennis at the **Messonghi Beach Hotel**.
❷ Between Moraitika and Messonghi ❶ 26610 83000 ❸ Courts open 06.00–21.00

Watersports and scuba diving
Learn to windsurf or sail a catamaran at **Wassersportstation** on the beach. You can also rent canoes and pedalos (❷ Moraitika ❶ 26610 75226). Or learn to scuba dive at the **Nautilus Diving School**, run by a friendly Anglo-Greek couple. Trips for qualified divers are also organised and equipment hire is available.

In the grounds of the Messonghi Beach Hotel, between Moraitika and Messonghi ☎ 26610 83045 ⓦ www.nautilusdivingcorfu.com ⏰ Office open 17.00–20.00

TAKING A BREAK

Fisherman's House ££ If you fancy a walk before dinner or lunch, stroll out to this charming taverna with pretty views across a tiny harbour. There's fresh fish daily. ⓐ Boukari Road, Messonghi ☎ 26610 75365 ⏰ 11.00–23.00

Rose Garden ££ Set back from the road in an attractive shady, very romantic garden. The *mezedes* here are something special – 16 different dishes of fried vegetables, dips and seafood. ⓐ Moraitika ☎ 26610 75622 ⏰ 18.00–01.00

Sparos ££ A small fish taverna set beneath trees and overlooking the sea. Friendly staff and good food make this a popular destination for fish lovers. ⓐ Boukari Road ⏰ 09.00–24.00

Spyros on the Beach ££ Now expanded to several beachfront terraces, Spyros has been serving fresh fish, Greek specials and English breakfasts to tourists since 1979. Try the homemade wine. ⓐ Messonghi beach, beside the river ☎ 26610 75285 ⏰ 08.00–24.00

AFTER DARK

Most nightlife options can be found along Moraitka's main road.

Barocco The best bar on the beach is brightly coloured with comfy sofas amidst wafting curtains. At night, candles are placed on the sand and there's a great vibe. There are over 100 cocktails on the menu; the Mojito house special will knock you over. ⓐ Messonghi beach ☎ 69326 60460 ⏰ 11.00–02.00

Captain Morgan's An English DJ keeps feet a-thumping and bodies a-jumping. ⓐ Moraitika ⓛ 19.00–02.00

Golden Beach A gaudy but popular bar with a large garden terrace, open-air dancing and Greek dancing shows every evening. ⓐ Moraitika beach ⓣ 26610 75564 ⓦ www.goldenbeachbar.com ⓛ 09.00–02.00

Oasis Bar Popular with British tourists, this bar has beer, cocktails, sports on big screens and a swimming pool that can be used by guests. ⓐ Central Messonghi ⓣ 69490 41584 ⓛ 10.00–03.00

Very CoCo A friendly club with a swimming pool and pool tables, and DJs with dancers on Saturdays. ⓐ Moraitika main road ⓣ 69370 34216 ⓛ 20.00–05.00, club from 24.00

SHOPPING
MORAITIKA
3Ks Shopping Centre A one-stop shop selling a wide range of toiletries, drinks and food. ⓣ 26610 76220 ⓛ 08.00–22.00
Efi's Leather Market As well as the usual selection of handbags, belts and wallets, Efi's shop also has a variety of soft leather coats and jackets, shoes and slippers. ⓣ 26610 75911 ⓛ 08.30–21.00

MESSONGHI
Handmade Ceramics shop This little shop has a fine array of bright and pastel ceramics, many of which are copies of ancient Greek statues and pottery. ⓛ 09.00–21.00
Natural Bakery A mouth-watering array of sticky *baklava*, doughnuts, cream cakes, *tiramisu* and a myriad of temptations for the sweet-toothed.
3Ks Similar to the supermarket in Moraitika, this large shop has everything from daily needs to traditional souvenirs and watersports equipment. ⓣ 26610 80305 ⓛ 08.00–24.00

Kavos

Stroll along Kavos' main street in the early evening and you could be in a ghost town. Do the same thing at 03.00 in the morning and you'll feel as if you've landed on another planet. Disco competes with house music and gaudy neon signs flash everywhere.

Bars are loud and full of cocktails with suggestive names – everything in Kavos is 'screaming' or 'multiple'. It's geared to the party market... it's brash, it's wild but it's also a huge amount of fun and one thing is for sure – you won't ever be bored.

On the northern fringes of Kavos, **St Peter's** is a quieter option, but still within easy reach of the action. There are watersports here, too, and a go-kart track and several beachside snack bars. You will find traditional Greek tavernas that also do great English breakfasts, pizza and pasta. Look out for all-inclusive menus which provide good value.

BEACHES

Kavos beach is sandy, over 2 km (1 mile) long, and shelves gently into the sea – the perfect place to gather your strength on the sandy beach while you plan the next evening's entertainment.

THINGS TO SEE & DO

Bungee jumping
Strictly for the fearless and the mad! Jump from a platform raised by a crane, or step in the Bungee Rocket and get launched up into the sky in a metal cage.
ⓐ Opposite The British Restaurant ⓛ 18.00–24.00

Cape Asprokavos walk
If you can tear yourself away from the bars and beach, an energetic 30-minute walk south takes you to the crumbling monastery of

Arkoudilas and the cliffs of Cape Asporkavos. It is worth it for the superb coastal views across to Paxos island. A boat trip from Kavos around Paxos (see page 93) is another option.

Watersports

Due to its very sheltered position, this is a great place for watersports. Try parasailing or scuba diving in the clear waters or go fast and furious in the *Crazy Speedboat*.

TAKING A BREAK

Pizza Garden £ The pizzas are enormous but don't worry if you can't eat it all, they'll box it up so you can take the rest home. ❶ 26620 61064 🕒 17.00–02.00

The Barn £ This fast-food place, part of the Barn complex, is usually at its busiest when clubbers in the grip of post-cocktail munchies come for a quick, cheap fix of hot dogs, burgers, chips or kebabs. ❸ Main road ❶ 26620 61332 🕒 19.00–04.00

The British Restaurant £ English food in large portions, served by friendly Greek waiters who break into a Greek dancing and plate-smashing routine most nights. Eat on the patio for a front-row view of the mad fools bungee jumping from the top of the crane opposite. ❸ Main road ❶ 26620 61488 🕒 08.00–24.00

Uncle Harry's £–££ Basic but tasty Greek and English food served on a large open veranda. ❸ Main road ❶ 26620 61173 🕒 10.00–23.00

AFTER DARK

Atlantis £ Who needs a hotel if you have this chilled-out, non-stop party venue right on the beach. Drink and dance your holiday away. Snacks served too. ❸ Kavos beach 🕒 24 hours

Futures A popular club, a mixture of tourists and locals dance and drink to house and rave music. It's the largest club in Kavos and top DJs from Ibiza take their turn at spinning the discs several times a summer. **ⓐ** Right in the middle of Kavos and easy to find **🕓** 23.00–04.00

Rockys Always busy, this open-air bar buzzes with a party atmosphere, fuelled by the special offers early on in the evening. A popular venue for UK DJs who keep the rowdy crowd happy till the early hours. **ⓐ** Main road **🕓** 20.00–06.00

S.E.X. A subtly named club famed for its 2 m (6 ft) deep foam parties. Join the happy crowd in the suds. **ⓐ** Main road **🕓** 01.00–06.00

The Rolling Stone A classic Kavos bar and club, home of lethal cocktails, poured straight into your mouth. Indie rock is played from 01.00. Just look for the well-known tongue sign. **ⓐ** Main road **🕓** 12.00–03.00

▲ *Sun loungers on Kavos beach*

Aghios Georgios (south-west)

This is part of the long, sandy stretch that fringes the whole south-west coastline of Corfu, framed by a backdrop of pine woods and olive trees, where you'll see the sign, 'Welcome to Corfu's best sandy beaches'. To the north of the resort are sand dunes and the saltwater lagoon. Nearby Lake Korission is a haven for wildlife, especially in the spring and autumn when it teems with migratory birds.

In Aghios Georgios itself, the more developed golden beaches have excellent watersports, perfect for all the family, and a good choice of tavernas overlooking the beach. There's a great selection of bars with quizzes, videos, bingo and karaoke, plus music and pool bars that buzz well into the small hours. Just inland is the traditional old Corfiot village of **Argirades**, worth a visit to see the lovely Venetian architecture and old monastery, or perhaps just to watch people and donkeys from a shaded café.

BEACHES

The most developed 'golden beach', offering a good range of watersports is at the southern end. There is a quiet beach a few minutes' walk north at Issos. The dunes north of here are the unofficial naturist area.

THINGS TO SEE & DO

Boat trips
Both Kostas and Captain Billy run regular day trips to Paxos, Antipaxos and the caves, and trips to Sivota and the Blue Lagoon on the Greek mainland three times weekly. Captain Billy additionally has trips to Paleokastritsa. Tickets can be booked at the harbour.

Birdwatching
Over 120 species of birds have been recorded as visitors to Lake Korissia, the lagoon just north of Aghios Georgios. Though most birds pass

through in the winter months, the lake still offers some sightings in summer. Be prepared for mosquitoes.

Watersports

Learn to parasail or water-ski, as there are all sorts of activities available here. **Nikos Sea Sports** is on the little port side of the beach. **Kosta's Jet Ski** is at the northern end of the beach, as is **Nautilus Diving**, a British Sub Aqua Club School with diving courses.

TAKING A BREAK

San Carlos £–££ Serving everything from breakfast to fresh fish and grilled dishes, this garden restaurant offers live music daily. ⓐ On the beach ① 26620 51186 ① 09.00–24.00

Zack's £–££ Paradise for the sweet-toothed, with delicious creamy cappuccinos, mouth-watering pastries and homemade ice creams. As a bonus, there's also a special play area for children. ⓐ Near the harbour ① 26620 52638 ① 12.00–23.00

Kafesas ££ Atmospheric taverna specialising in traditional Corfiot dishes and serving only organic food and homemade wine and bread. The hospitable owner, Akis, and his wife, Miriam, have three fishing boats to supply them with the freshest fish, lobster, crab and mussels. Visit the kitchen to see what's cooking today. There are over 100 different *mezedes* to choose from. ⓐ Southern end of the resort ① 26620 51196 ① 09.00–02.00 ① Book ahead for the Greek dancing nights on Fri & Sat

Panorama ££ Good Greek and international food served in a garden overlooking the sea – you can see all the way to Paxos island in good weather. ⓐ Ag. Georgios beach ① 22620 52352 ① 09.00–23.00

Sea Gull ££ A lovely villa set in a green garden houses this restaurant with sea view. Try the grilled meat or fish dishes here. ⓐ Main road, southern side of the resort ⓣ 26620 51204 ⓛ 18.00–01.00

AFTER DARK

La Perla Corfu's only original hippie hangout. This scruffy wooden den of a bar has occasional art exhibitions and live music, and its chilled-out music is great to relax to. ⓐ Main road ⓛ Sunset to sunrise

Traxx Very popular bar with football on the big screen, quiz and karaoke nights. ⓐ Next to Golden Sands Hotel

Easy Busy £–££ This lively pub with a family-friendly atmosphere is a home from home for many regulars, and good value too. ⓐ Near the harbour ⓣ 69727 79527 ⓛ 14.00–02.00

Reflections & Stamatis Bar ££ Newly renovated in 2007, this large disco is the resort's most popular, playing music till the sun comes up. The pleasant Stamatis Bar attached to it is a great place to enjoy a fish or other Greek meal and to warm up for the dancing action.
ⓐ Main road ⓣ 22620 52098 ⓛ 10.00–05.00

SHOPPING
Dolphins Shop This shop sells high-quality ceramics and museum copies created by local artist Katerina, whose special passion is dolphins. She also runs a small gold and silver craft shop full of handmade designs, just across the street from the gift shop.
ⓐ Near the port ⓣ 26620 53022 ⓛ 09.30–23.00

Aghios Gordios

At Aghios Gordios you will find one of the island's most beautiful beaches, with fascinating rock formations and sheer cliffs plunging into the sea. Headlands, hills, silvery olive groves and sandy stretches of soft golden sand with patches of shingle frame the crystal-clear blue waters.

Dominating the bay off the southern headland is a gigantic rock which resembles a tusk, called the **Ortholith**. At the northern end are **Plitri Point** and the rocky pinnacles of **Aerostatos** – formerly known as 'The Sentry' to keep a look-out for invaders and pirates. Bathing here is very safe and the resort has one of the island's best beaches for children. The rocks at either end are excellent for snorkelling and spear-fishing and the resort is highly popular with watersports enthusiasts.

THINGS TO SEE & DO

Cliffs of Aerostato
For a stunning view of the coastline from the top of the cliffs, head 600 m (650 yds) uphill through the forest from the northern end of the village. There's a taverna here, too.

Sinarades
Just inland to the north of Aghios Gordios is this charming hill village, where winding streets lead past traditional old houses with flowers tumbling in bright profusion, to a lovely square with a fountain, shaded by tall palm trees – the meeting place for the locals. It's a good place to enjoy a drink before following the signs up the alleyway to the excellent **Folk Museum of Central Corfu** inside a Corfiot village house, and a time-capsule of the 19th century. It has a fine collection of local historical artefacts and offers a rare glimpse into a vanishing way of life. Highlights are the lovely Asian-style shadow puppets and the parts of a World War II bomber plane shot down nearby.

🅐 2 Nikokavoura ☎ 26610 54962 🕐 09.30–14.00 Mon–Sat ❶ Admission charge. The six daily buses between Aghios Gordios and Corfu Town pass through Sinarades.

Watersports

Try **Calypso Diving** to learn how to dive or practise your skills in the superb waters around here, perfect for diving.

🅐 300 m (328 yds) on the right past the Romantic Palace Restaurant (☎ 26610 53101 🌐 www.calypso-diving.gr). **Kosta's** has facilities for a wide range of watersports.

🅐 On the beach in front of Sea Breeze Taverna

TAKING A BREAK

Ark £ A small wooden music bar overlooking the beach. Relax and enjoy the view with some snacks and drinks, or come on Saturday nights to dance. 🅐 Ag. Gordios beach ☎ 26610 53480 🕐 10.00–03.00 🌐 www.ark.gr

Alobar £–££ A friendly lounge bar and club with Greek and international snacks, drinks and good cocktails. One of the few happening night places along the beach, with regular live music. 🅐 Ag. Gordios beach ☎ 26610 53997 🕐 11.00–02.00

> ### SHOPPING
> **Olive Wood Shop** All kinds of bowls and carvings crafted in luxuriant olive wood as well as a delightful selection of wind-chimes, silver frames, icons and modern jewellery. 🅐 Main road ☎ 26610 53939 🕐 10.00–14.30 & 17.30–23.00; evening only Sun
> **Venus** Good-quality silver frames, icons and stylish modern jewellery in this Aladdin's cave. 🅐 Next door to the Olive Wood Shop ☎ 26610 53939 🕐 10.00–14.30 & 17.30–23.00 Mon–Sat, 17.30–23.00 Sun

Sea Breeze Taverna ££ All manner of Greek specialities, barbecues and regular Greek nights and dancing make this a very popular venue in an excellent location. There's even a playground for the children. ⓐ On the beach ⓣ 26610 53214 ⓛ 09.00–01.00

Sebastian ££ Good homemade Greek and international food and Corfiot specialities served on an atmospheric wide terrace. Special fish nights and barbecues. Make sure you sample the good homemade wines, in every colour, too. Does regular and spectacular Greek nights. ⓐ Just off the main road ⓣ 26610 53256 ⓛ 09.00–24.00

The Mad Greek ££ Shaded by palm trees, this family-run and orientated restaurant has been going since 1994, serving steaks, fresh fish and Greek dishes. ⓐ Situated on a small street off the main road ⓣ 26610 53743 ⓛ 17.00–23.30

Theodoros ££ The oldest taverna in the resort was set up by the Dukakis brothers in the 1960s when the first tourists arrived – and it's been a success ever since. Excellent Greek home cooking and fresh fish available. ⓐ Ag. Gordios beach ⓣ 26610 53259 ⓛ 09.00–23.00

Zephyros ££ Be seated on wooden terraces in a beautiful flower-filled garden overlooking the beach, and sample affordable *mezedes* and Greek specialities. ⓐ Ag. Gordios beach ⓣ 26610 59079 ⓛ 11.30–23.30

Glyfada & Pelekas

Glyfada's long swathe of golden sand ranks amongst the best beaches on the island. The road down to the resort winds through olive groves to the bluest of shallow waters, sheltered by steep cliffs at either end. Several tavernas line the beach that is much sought after for watersports as well as for swimming in the crystal-clear sea.

BEACHES

To the north lies **Myrtiotissa**, which was described by Lawrence Durrell in *Prospero's Cell* as 'perhaps the loveliest beach in the world', nowadays known (unofficially) as the island's naturist beach and a paradise for snorkellers. Best visited by boat, there are plenty of excursions and water-taxis from the surrounding area. Once there, you will find a beach bar and a tiny 14th-century monastery, dedicated to Our Lady of the Myrtles.

To the south of Glyfada is **Pelekas**, whose long, sandy beach also attracts some naturists – but is best known for its excellent swimming and fabulous vantage points from the hilltop village inland. 'Kaiser's Lookout (Throne)' is the panoramic viewpoint much frequented by Kaiser Wilhelm II from his **Achilleion Palace** (see page 86). This was his favourite spot on the island and he built a special telescope tower here to see his beloved sunsets more intimately. There are shops, tavernas and cafés clustered around the village and an excellent, sandy beach, accessible by car down a narrow, winding road.

THINGS TO SEE & DO

Watersports

Every manner of watersport is available from the beaches at Glyfada and Pelekas, among them parasailing, water-skiing, windsurfing and sailing. Around Glyfada beach you will find companies that run all sorts of watersport activities as well as hiring out motorboats by the hour, so you can explore the neighbouring beaches.

For a special treat take a full-day boat trip from Glyfada in a trimaran, all-inclusive of lunch and drinks, or indulge in a moonlit romantic trip (pricey but worth it).

TAKING A BREAK

Aloha Beach Club £–££ Breakfast, lunch and delicious *mezedes* in the evening with wine from the barrel. Latin-American and reggae music, with dancing until late. ⓐ Glyfada, in the middle of the beach
ⓣ 26610 94380 ⓒ 09.00–23.00

Golden Beach Restaurant & Bar £–££ A great beachside location, this taverna specialises in fresh fish but also serves snacks throughout the day. Try the delicious swordfish. ⓐ Glyfada beach, southern side
ⓣ 26610 94223 ⓒ 09.00–23.00 Mon–Sat

● *View across Glyfada down to the beach*

Jimmy's £–££ Authentic Corfiot and Greek cuisine served in a friendly family taverna and guesthouse. ⓐ Pelekas village ❶ 26610 94284 🕑 08.30–23.00 ⓦ www.jimmyspelekas.com

Spiros Taverna £–££ Fresh fish is the speciality here, overlooking the sea. Delicious squid and lobster and good value snacks served all day in high season. ⓐ Pelekas beach ❶ 26610 94641 🕑 08.30–23.00

Taverna Glyfada Beach £–££ Family-run bar and taverna serving good Greek specialities and fish – look out for the catch of the day. Lovely setting right on the northern end of the beach. ⓐ Glyfada beach ❶ 26610 94487 🕑 10.00–23.00

Banana Club ££ Great atmosphere in this hilltop setting with all kinds of music from jazz and ethnic to the sounds of today. ⓐ On Pelekas Road to Kaiser's Lookout 🕑 17.00–24.00

Gorgona ££ Delicious Greek specialities and fresh fish in a pleasant, friendly environment. ⓐ Glyfada beach, southern end ❶ 26610 94336 🕑 07.00–23.00

Figareto ££–£££ The main restaurant of the luxurious Louis Grand Hotel serves good buffets – eat as much as you like for a fixed price on the panoramic terrace. The hotel has several other comfortable bars and restaurants with superb views across the sandy beach. Perfect for a special occasion. ⓐ Southern end of Glyfada beach ❶ 26610 94140 🕑 18.30–21.30

Sunset Restaurant ££–£££ Lovely terrace with stunning views – especially at sunset. Part of the luxury Sunset Hotel with both Greek and international specialities to match. ⓐ Located high up by Kaiser's Lookout, about 3 km (2 miles) from Pelekas ❶ 26610 94230 🕑 09.00–23.00

Ermones

Picturesque little Ermones lies between two steep headlands which tumble down from the fertile Ropa Valley. According to legend, Homer's Odysseus was washed ashore here in a state of exhaustion after his ten-year voyage home from the Trojan Wars. He was found by the beautiful Nausicaa who had come to wash clothes with her handmaidens at a nearby stream – said to be that of Paleokastritsa or Ermones and its beach. He was given shelter and then eventually returned home to his native island of Ithaca.

The Ropa river flows out to the sea at Ermones, which has a fine shingle and sand beach and flies a Blue Flag. The sea is beautifully clear, excellent for snorkelling, and there are numerous watersports on offer. There's also a safe rock pool for children – perfect for crabbing.

THINGS TO SEE & DO

Golf

Corfu's only golf club, **The Corfu Golf and Country Club**, is just inland from Ermones in the Ropa Valley. This famous 18-hole course is 6 km (4 miles) long with a par of 72 and has been described as one of the greatest courses in Europe. It certainly has a few challenges with water hazards and a design making it more like a links course, and is very popular with

⬤ *Enjoy the beach in Ermones*

golfers from all over the island. Clubs are available for hire and you can get lessons with qualified pros. Good shop, clubhouse with bar and restaurant at the 19th hole.

ⓐ Ropa Valley ⓣ 26610 94220 ⓦ www.corfugolfclub.com

Horse riding

The Ropa Valley just above Ermones is one of the most beautiful and fertile areas of the island. Here you can ride amongst fig, pear and apple trees and through vineyards which stretch for miles. Ponies and horses are available from **Ropa Valley Riding Stables** for both novice and experienced riders. Rides are for approximately two hours with a stop for refreshments.

ⓐ On the approach road to Ermones ⓣ 26610 94220

Local wines

There are some good wines on Corfu, though they're often hard to find. The best (and most expensive) bottled wine is Theotoki, produced from the grapes of the Ropa Valley near Ermones. You can't visit the winery, but some of its wines are available locally on Corfu – a good change from the usual house wine.

Watersports

Odyssey Divers offers fantastic scuba diving from the beach in crystal-clear waters which shelve quickly into the deep.

ⓐ On the beach ⓣ 26610 94241

EXCURSION
Aqualand

Get 'Wet 'n' Wild' at Aqualand which has to be one of the best water adventure parks in Greece. Ride the Kamikaze, plunge into the Black Hole, twirl around the Crazy River, relax in the Lazy River, then attempt the Slippery Frog, Hydrotube, Four Twisters, a quick whirl in the Big Jacuzzi® – before starting all over again! There are also slides of all sizes, a games arcade, a 'wet and dry' bar, bouncing castle and children's pool.

This is an excellent day out for all the family and the admission price – quite high – includes everything, from the rides and all facilities to the use of sunbeds and parasols around the pools. The well-stocked souvenir shop, boutique, bars, ice cream parlour and restaurants are, of course, extra. It's extremely popular and attracts visitors from all over the island.

🅐 Aqualand is at Aghios Ioannis on the Pelekas to Ermones road
🅣 26610 52963/58351 🅦 www.aqualand-corfu.com 🅛 10.00–18.00 May–Oct; 10.00–19.00 July & Aug ❶ Admission charge

TAKING A BREAK

Dizzy's Music Café Bar £ Music from the 1960s to Latin American and reggae, right up to today, which makes for a great atmosphere.
🅐 Next to the Sunmarotel Calimera Ermones Beach 🅛 17.00–24.00

George's Taverna £–££ Fresh fish is the speciality here with lobster on request – best to reserve in advance. Or try the delicious *mezedes* – meals in themselves. 🅣 26610 94506 🅛 09.00–24.00

Maria's Taverna £–££ The owner Spiros makes you welcome here at this adjoining taverna to George's with the same beautiful views over the sea. The food's pretty good too! 🅣 26610 94659 🅛 09.00–24.00

Nafsica £–££ Brothers George and Nikos extend a warm welcome to this beachside taverna where good Corfiot specialities and delicious red mullet feature amongst the fresh fish on the menu. Greek dancing twice a week with live music. 🅐 Part of the Ermones Golf Hotel 🅣 26610 94236 🅛 09.00–23.00

Sunmarotel Ermones Beach ££–£££ This hotel dominates the little bay of Ermones. A funicular railway runs down from the hotel to the beach, and a ride on this will take you to the good restaurant which serves Corfiot specialities and fresh seafood. 🅐 Ermones beach
🅣 26610 94241 🅛 08.00–24.00

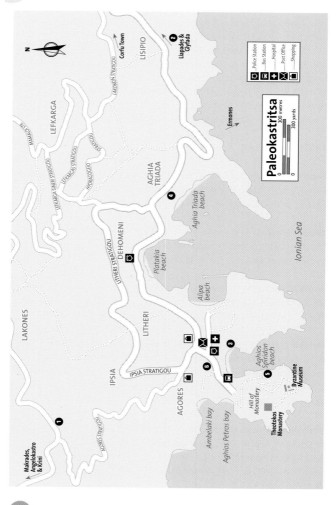

Paleokastritsa

Picturesque Paleokastritsa sits above a craggy coastline below densely wooded hillsides. The sea is particularly refreshing here, as it's one of the coolest spots on the island. Apart from offering sheltered beaches, it's a great base for nearby excursions, such as Liapades with its beach and dramatic backdrop of cliffs, or the castle at Angelokastro.

BEACHES

The white-pebbled **Aghia Triada beach** at the eastern end of the village is one of the largest, and is popular with families. The two neighbouring beaches, **Platakia** and **Alipa**, are rather quieter. Trendy young teenagers head for the sandy strip at **Aghios Spiridon**. The smaller **Aghios Petros** and **Ambelaki bays** lie on the western side of the peninsula. If you're in the area for more than one day, sail along the coast of Liapades and visit **Stelari beach**, which is accessible only by boat.

THINGS TO SEE & DO

Angelokastro
Angelokastro, a ruined 13th-century fortress that stands on a rocky cliff near the village of Krini, was originally built to defend Corfu from pirate raids in Byzantine times. The views are unrivalled, with a 360° panorama over the craggy coastline and the Theotokos Monastery.

Boating
It's easy to join a boating day trip or to use a water-taxi to get to quiet beaches between here and Ermones. A good short trip is to the **Blue Eye Cave** (Cave of Nausicaa) – rumoured to be where Odysseus met Nausicaa in Homer's ancient Greek epic. You can also rent a boat and zip around the caves and beaches yourself. Three companies around Aghios Spiridon bay rent out self-drive boats: **Kahlua** (☎ 39774 09246), **Sea Foam Safari** (☎ 69757 80000) and **Skiclub** 105 (☎ 69766 50175).

Diving

Paleokastritsa's bays and rock formations are excellent for snorkelling and diving. Do a beginners' try dive or a full PADI course with Achilleon Diving.

☎ 26610 95350 ⓦ www.diving-corfu.com

Lakones

Take the path (signposted to Lakones) to the left of the Odysseus Hotel. After about 45 minutes, you'll come out into the back alleyways of

⬥ *A mural at Theotokos Monastery*

Lakones with its jumble of whitewashed houses. The **Café Olympia**, on the main road, is a good place for a drink. From here, head west along the coastal road to the Bella Vista for a wonderful panoramic view over the monastery and the sparkling sapphire sea. You'll pass an olive wood workshop where you can see a local craftsman painstakingly shaping the wood.

Liapades

Liapades has delightful old Venetian manor houses and courtyards, narrow twisting lanes and a lovely church. Wizened old men sit nodding sagely in the village square as women, riding side-saddle, trundle past on their donkeys after long mornings working in the vineyards.

Theotokos Monastery

Located on a headland jutting out into the sea, this 13th-century monastery is home to a few monks. The small church has a beautiful ceiling and the tiny icon museum has the skeleton of a sea monster – really a small whale – found in 1860. The views from the pretty garden are stunning. Shawls and skirts are available for underdressed tourists.
🕿 26630 41210 🕐 07.00–13.00 & 15.00–20.00 ❶ Admission free; donations welcome

TAKING A BREAK

Golden Fox £–££ ❶ Built on the mountainside offering magnificent views of the sheltered bays of Paleokastritsa and the Ionian Sea. This family-run restaurant, part of a complex offering accommodation, a bar and swimming pool, offers delicious homemade food and pastries. ⓐ Just outside Lakones ❶ 26630 49101 ❷ 09.00–23.00

Michalis £–££ ❷   A good selection of Greek specialities and international dishes are served at bargain prices. A four-course set-price menu will set you back very little, and there is plenty of choice for children. ⓐ Entrance to old village of Liapades on the way up from the beach ❶ 26630 41178 ❷ 10.00–23.00

Smurf's ££ ❸   Atmospheric Greek taverna beside the beach and car park, with good views, fresh fish and lobster for you to select from tanks, and good Corfiot specialities. ⓐ Aghios Spiridon beach ❶ 26630 41358 ❷ 09.00–24.00

Poseidon Beach ££–£££ ❹   By the sea, and an excellent, relaxing place to stop off. Serves good local food and fish too. ⓐ Aghia Triada beach ❶ 26630 41225 ❷ 08.30–24.00

Vrachos £££ ❺   Enjoy fresh fish while relaxing at this good family restaurant. The shaded terrace offers good views of the bay. ⓐ Aghios Spiridon bay, at the foot of the monastery hill ❶ 26630 41233 ❷ 09.00–23.00

AFTER DARK

Apollon ££ ❻   It's not just the air-conditioning that makes this Paleokastritsa's coolest bar. Whether you come during the day from snacks and Greek meals, or drop by in the evening for beer and cocktails, there's always a chilled-out atmosphere here. ⓐ Aghios Spiridon beach ❶ 26630 41211 ❷ 08.00–03.00

Aghios Georgios (north-west)

The south-facing bay at Aghios Georgios stretches for over 3 km (2 miles) and is backed by statuesque cypress trees and olive groves. The beach has a Blue Flag, awarded for its pristine beach and clear sea, which is excellent for all kinds of watersports, especially for windsurfing.

THINGS TO SEE & DO

Walking

Take a walk around the bay to the quiet little village of Afionas, which sits on top of Cape Arillas, the northern part of Aghios Georgios bay. The path from the village square leads you down to a glorious panoramic outlook with views to the west towards the island of Kravia. From here you can follow the steepish footpath on to the cape. Below there are two secluded little shingle beaches which are excellent for snorkelling.

Watersports

Diving Fun Club The glorious scenery above the surface of the sea is matched by the natural beauty under the sea. For beginners and experienced dives alike.

☎ 26630 96092 **Ⓦ** www.corfudivingfunclub.gr

SunFun Club Caters for most water activities from paragliding to hiring your own motorboat or taking water-taxis to the neighbouring beaches.

☎ 26630 96355

TAKING A BREAK

Blue Heaven ££ A lovely, modern restaurant overlooking the sea in the northern part of the resort. Try some fresh fish or go for other Greek and international dishes. **ⓐ** Beachfront **☎** 26630 96220 **Ⓛ** 09.00–01.00

Delfini ££ Big terrace overlooking the sea with a bird's-eye view of the windsurfing school, serving breakfasts, snacks, pizzas and excellent *mezedes* as well as fresh fish. ⓐ Beach road ❶ 26630 96323 ❷ 09.00–23.00

Fisherman's Cabin ££ A long-established favourite, with seating around an enormous olive tree in the middle of a garden. It specialises in fish of all kinds, including Corfiot specialities; try the prawns cooked in *ouzo*. Drive along the bumpy track to get there, or walk there in 30–45 minutes (bring a torch to get back to the resort in the dark!). ⓐ Southern beachfront ❶ 69425 85550 ❷ 16.00–23.00, 13.30–23.00 Sat and Sun

Vrachos ££ A great place for lobster and crayfish, which are on the menu every day. You're guaranteed a warm welcome from the owner, Kostas, on his restaurant terrace, as well as gorgeous views across the bay. Also serves Corfiot specialities such as *sofrito* (see page 97), all manner of fresh fish, and good hamburgers. ⓐ Northern beachfront ❶ 26630 96373 ❷ 09.00–23.00

Akrogiali ££–£££ Excellent fish restaurant down a small track at the southern end of the resort. Push the boat out with specialities such as lobster spaghetti, or try the less expensive Bourdeto (fish stew). ⓐ Southern beachfront ❶ 69773 34278 ❷ 12.00–23.00

AFTER DARK

Balloon Club Aghios Georgios' disco has good dance music from the 60s right up to today, played by lively DJs. The action starts winding up in the late evening until the small hours. ⓐ Resort centre, inland beyond the bridge ❷ 23.00–06.00 Wed–Sun

Arillas

The mainly sandy, Blue Flag beach shelves very gently into the shallow turquoise sea, making this an ideal spot for families. Lying at the northern end of a long bay, the setting is spectacular with a lovely backdrop of green hills and olive groves, and excellent views of the little island of Kravia (known as 'Ship Island') to the south.

THINGS TO SEE & DO

Watersports
Arillas Watersports Parasails, water-skis, windsurf boards, pedaloes and canoes are all available for hire here.
ⓐ Kiosk on the beach

Flamingo This is a free freshwater swimming pool – relax with a drink beside the pool. There is also a happy hour.
ⓐ Beachfront, near Porto Fino

TAKING A BREAK

Graziella £–££ A large family restaurant with a terrace looking across the sea. Aris, the owner, assures you of a warm welcome and good-value menus, and fresh fish is the speciality. ⓐ Seafront ❶ 26630 51039 🕐 12.00–23.00

Arillas Inn ££ Relax under the vine-covered terrace and enjoy a long cool drink – perhaps an iced coffee – or feast on lobster, steaks or *mezedes*.

> **SHOPPING**
> **Ina's Tourist and Gift Shop** Sells 'designer' T-shirts, wraps and sarongs, all at good prices. ⓐ Beachfront, next to Horizon Hotel

🔺 *Sunbeds await sun worshippers in Arillas*

There's also Greek dancing and plate smashing every Wednesday.
ⓐ Beachfront ⓣ 26630 51070 ⓒ 09.00–23.00

Marina ££ This shaded terrace with seaview has a welcoming atmosphere and serves Greek specialities, fresh fish and delicious grilled lobster. Drop by on Saturdays for the Greek night, with Corfiot dances.
ⓐ Beachfront, Marina Hotel ⓣ 26630 51100 ⓒ 08.30–23.00

AFTER DARK

Coconut Bar By day a quiet bar where the staff will be happy to chat, by night a lively cocktail bar serving over 100 cocktails as DJs play sounds to bop around to. ⓐ Main street ⓣ 26630 51150 ⓒ 10.00–03.00

Malibu A buzzing cocktail bar with TV screens for sports and karaoke, and a DJ spinning classic rock songs till late. ⓐ Main street ⓣ 26630 51243 ⓦ www.malibu-arillas.com ⓒ 09.00–04.00

Aghios Stefanos

A wide stretch of sand sweeps round a sparkling bay enclosed on one side by cliffs and on the other by the red-roofed village nestling on the hills. Best of all, it's quiet and peaceful. The resort is a haven for seekers of tranquility – there is nothing more restful than watching the fishing boats return in the afternoon. However, despite being so low-key, there are plenty of quality tavernas and a couple of venues where the dancing continues until the small hours.

THINGS TO SEE & DO

Arillas
Walk to the village of Arillas (page 49) for lunch or dinner at one of the seaside tavernas (as for the chapel but turn left at the top). The stroll there is flower-strewn, fragrant and filled with birds and butterflies, while crickets sing in the undergrowth. The panorama over the bay at San Stefanos and the narrow beach at Arillas is stunning. Paths are rough and uneven – flat shoes are a good idea.

Boating
Take a sunbathing, sightseeing and swimming boat trip to the attractive Diapontia islands – Mathraki, Othoni and Ereikoussa – off the north-western coast. Nearhos does daily boat trips from the small harbour.

Parasailing
Go parasailing with Captain Niko's Watersports (ⓐ beachfront kiosk). You can go alone or with a friend – tandem rides are fun and save money too.

Tennis
Courts are available for rent near the Perros apartments, with lessons for beginners. Go to the house opposite the courts, no 168, for information.

Walking

Take a walk up to the 18th-century **Aghios Stefanos chapel** at the southernmost point of the bay. You can either follow the track alongside the Hotel Nafsica's pool or, for a gentler climb, take the path opposite the **Summer Dream restaurant**. The walk up affords lovely views over the beach and hills beyond. Try to make the trip towards the end of the day when the wild thyme and jasmine perfumes of the Mediterranean *maquis* are at their strongest.

TAKING A BREAK

Mango Beach Bar £–££ Set above the beach with views over the sea and the village harbour, Mango is a great place to base yourself for a day; sunbeds and parasols are for rent and in the bar there are cool drinks and ice cream, as well as full Greek and international meals.
ⓐ Beachfront ● 09.00–23.00

Waves £–££ A simple beachside taverna with a good selection of snacks and meals to keep you out of the sun during the hottest hours of the day. Greek dishes, ice cream and drinks are available. ⓐ Beachfront, near the harbour ● 09.00–23.00

Elpida's Bistro ££ The taverna at Nondas Apartments, a short walk uphill from the beach, is a lovely place for a romantic dinner with a view over the bay. Dimitri and Nicki serve up good Greek and Mediterranean dishes here with jazz and blues music on the speakers. Children's menu too.
ⓐ Aghios Stefanos village ✆ 26630 51808 ● 12.00–23.00

Manthos ££ The oldest taverna in the resort dates back to 1976 and serves up excellent traditional Greek food, with simple dishes for children. Specialities include tender chargrilled chicken, and barbecued braised beef. ⓐ Main road ❶ 26630 52197 🕓 12.00–24.00

Mistral ££ The tempting aroma of barbecued meat mingles with the sea breeze on Mistral's beachside patio. Later in the evening, watch the waiters juggle burning tables in their fire dance. ⓐ Main road ❶ 26630 52072 🕓 09.00–24.00

Nafsika ££ Service here is professional and the menu is peppered with unusual dishes as well as Greek and international staples. Varied and tasty range for vegetarians too; try the stuffed vine leaves or fresh pitta bread with four dips. ⓐ Main road ❶ 26630 51051 🕓 09.00–24.00

Sunset Taverna ££ This is a family-orientated restaurant with regular fun Greek nights. Sample the popular speciality lamb gastra, lamb cooked in a mix of herbs, on the rose-filled terrace or enjoy the lovely views up into the hills. ⓐ Main road ❶ 26630 51185 🕓 09.00–23.00

AFTER DARK

Athens Bar £ Go with the flow at this wacky and fun bar. The staff are always joking and full of life and the music reflects the mood of the clientele, sometimes rocking to reggae, at others dancing wildly to house. Snacks and simple meals are available too. ⓐ Avlioton ❶ 26630 51764 ⓦ www.athens-bar.com 🕓 09.00–03.00

Condor Club ££ A varied crowd gathers in the large front bar for dinner and cocktails, quizzes and bingo. At midnight, locals and holidaymakers, young and old, head to the spacious club at the back to dance the night away. ⓐ Northern road ❶ 26630 95438 🕓 10.00–04.00

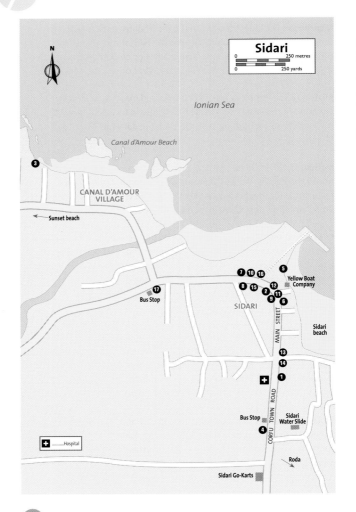

Sidari

0 — 250 metres
0 — 250 yards

Ionian Sea

Canal d'Amour Beach

3

CANAL D'AMOUR VILLAGE

← Sunset beach

SIDARI

7 **10** **16**

5

Yellow Boat Company

8 **15** **12**

2

9 **11**

6

17
Bus Stop

MAIN STREET

Sidari beach

13

14

1

✚

Sidari Water Slide

Bus Stop

CORFU TOWN ROAD

4

→ Roda

✚ ....Hospital

Sidari Go-Karts

Sidari

Days spent in Sidari are sleepy and languid, with nothing more demanding than lazing on the beach, paddling about on a pedalo or sitting in the shade of one of the many beach bars. Come the evening, the atmosphere fast-forwards to vibrant and lively. The hardest choice you'll have to make, though, is which restaurant to choose and whether to take to the stage in a karaoke performance or simply dance until dawn.

BEACHES

Sidari beach stretches the entire length of the main road, a long sweep of dark terracotta sand lapped by warm, shallow water. A ten-minute walk away at the western end of the beach there are several sandy coves enclosed by rocky gorges. Named Canal d'Amour ('channel of love') after a naturally eroded tunnel through one of the cliffs, tourist myth had it that swimming through it guaranteed a lifetime of love with your dream partner, but unfortunately the tunnel has since collapsed and you'll have to try your luck in one of the discos instead! **Sunset beach**, about 3 km (2 miles) west of Sidari, is one of the best spots in Corfu to watch the sun set. The setting is spectacular – a narrow strip of sand set at the bottom of sheer cliffs.

THINGS TO SEE & DO

Bowling

The modern Sidari Bowling Centre has two lanes, as well as a bar, pool tables, internet café, arcade games and a children's corner.
ⓐ Main road ⓣ 26630 95531 ⓛ 10.00–01.30

By bike or horse

Hire a mountain bike for the day and go as you please. The energetic can take a 12-km (7¹/₂-mile) guided cycle tour through quiet country lanes and olive groves. Alternatively, let the horse take the strain whilst you enjoy the scenery. Visit **Mountain Mania**, or the **Yellow Boat Company** office (see below).

Go-karting

Hit the tracks at **Sidari Go-Karts**, near the BP garage. Adults can choose low- or high-powered karts according to their kamikaze tendencies and ability. Mini karts are available for children under five.

Horse carriage rides

Enjoy a romantic trot around town in a white horse carriage. Find them parked at the western end of the main road from 19.00.

Watersports

Explore the northern coastline in a self-driven motorboat. Contact the **Yellow Boat Company** on the beach or at the office in the small shopping mall on the main street.

🕐 26630 95555 ❶ No permit required

🔺 *Surfing in Sidari*

Spend a day at **Sidari Water Slide**. The kids will love splashing about in the pool and playing on the slides. Tickets are inexpensive, sunbeds and umbrellas free. There's a snack bar serving sandwiches, spaghetti and drinks.

ⓐ Corfu Town Road ⓣ 26630 99066 ⓛ 10.00–19.00

TAKING A BREAK

Sweet Desire £ ❶ An excellent bakery shop and supermarket, with a small seating area if you can't wait to gobble down the delicious homemade cakes, pastries and sticky baklava. ⓐ Corfu Town Road ⓣ 26630 95596 ⓛ 08.00–23.00

Bolero £–££ ❷ Large portions of English food and a few Corfiot specialities are served in this pub-cum-garden bar with interesting choices for vegetarians and kids. Come 22.00, the decades roll back to the 1960s and 1970s and would-be pop stars sing their hearts out in the nightly karaoke sessions. ⓐ Main Street ⓣ 26630 95244 ⓛ 09.00–01.00

Aquarius ££ ❸ Near the Canal d'Amour, this poolside restaurant has good Greek and international food and great views of the sea. ⓐ Canal d'Amour area ⓣ 26630 99401 ⓛ 09.00–23.00

SHOPPING
Olive Wood House Small shop with a wide range of carved objects. ⓐ Corfu Town Road ⓣ 26610 45657 ⓛ 09.00–23.00
The Pottery Shop A large selection of ceramics, including original museum copies. ⓐ Main Street ⓛ 10.00–23.00
Tassos and Bill A reasonable selection of belts, wallets and bags, but the real bargains are the fur-lined slippers, in the softest suede, and the leather gloves. ⓐ Main Street ⓛ 09.00–23.00

Captain's ££ ❹   A simple restaurant serving fresh fish as well as pasta and steaks. A bit out of town along the road. ⓐ Corfu Town Road ❶ 26630 95568 ❷ 16.00–03.00

Elysee ££ ❺   The owner, Takis, gives you a warm welcome to this family restaurant, which serves breakfast, snacks, main dishes and ice cream. ⓐ On the beachfront ❷ 09.00–02.00

Hawaii ££ ❻   Greek home cooking, fresh fish and mouth-watering ice creams in this grillroom bar. ⓐ Main Street ❶ 26630 95195

Magic Wok ££ ❼   A nicely decorated rooftop Chinese and Asian restaurant with great views over the beach. Good-value set meals and specials for children too. ⓐ Main Street, above Bed Bar ❶ 26630 99449 ❷ 16.30–24.00

Pancho's Villa ££ ❽   An airy first-floor restaurant serving Tex-Mex dishes on a terrace overlooking the crowds on the main street. Wear a silly hat and try the 'booming burrito' or the 'chunky chimichanga' for a taste of Mexico. ⓐ Main Street ❶ 26630 95414 ❷ 17.00–24.00

Olympic ££–£££ ❾   Dine on the lovely rear terrace at Sidari's oldest taverna, under a canopy of jasmine flowers. If you like to people-watch, the seating at the front overlooks the main street. ⓐ Main Street ❶ 26630 95945 ❷ 09.00–24.00

AFTER DARK

Bed Bar ❿   One of the most popular nightlife venues in Sidari, this beachside New York-style 'beverage, entertainment, dining' venue has funky lounge furniture, air-conditioning, regular parties, English DJs and entertainment shows. ⓐ Main Street ❶ 26630 99449 ⓦ www.bedbar.gr ❷ 10.00–02.00

Caesar's ⑪ Sidari's best disco holds up to 1,500 revellers and blasts out dance music till the early hours. Apart from excellent resident DJs, there are often visiting DJs from abroad. ⓐ Main Street ⏱ 23.00–06.00

Faros ⑫ A restaurant and beach bar during the day, Faros transforms into a dance bar by night with a fun atmosphere and every disco classic since the 1960s played by English DJs. ⓐ Main Street ☎ 26630 95012 ⏱ 10.00–06.00 ❗ Admission charge after 23.00, look for free-entry fliers handed out on the beach

IQ Bar ⑬ Despite the name, your IQ is not going to be tested at this music and cocktail bar decorated with old LPs, but you'll probably leave dizzier and happier. ⓐ Main Street ☎ 26630 95635 ⏱ 10.00–02.30

Mojo ⑭ This relaxed music bar on the corner of the main crossing in town is great for watching the appalling driving habits of the locals and tourists, while downing a few beers or cocktails. There's regular live rock and Indie music. ⓐ Main Street ☎ 26630 95039 ⏱ 11.00–03.00

Shakers ⑮ A well-designed bar serving food and drinks all day. By night the music is turned up and there's a good atmosphere for chatting and dancing. ⓐ Main Street ☎ 26630 95756 ⏱ 10.00–05.00

SOS Bar ⑯ A first-floor bar attracting a mixed crowd for the cocktails and energy drink specials. On Thursdays there's live rock music. ⓐ Main Street ⏱ 18.00–04.00

Theo and Billy's Cocktail Bar ⑰ All ages can enjoy the lively atmosphere of this entertaining pub. There's bingo, pool, video games, satellite and Sky TV, or you can just relax over a cocktail whilst the DJ plays jazz, blues and up-to-date dance music at a civilised level. ⓐ Near the bus stop, Main Street ☎ 26630 95054 ⏱ 17.00–01.00

Roda

Once a quiet fishing village, Roda has become a favourite with families who love the long sand-and-pebble beach and safe, shallow water. There are plenty of pretty walks, watersports, pony treks and excursions.

THINGS TO SEE & DO

Coastal road
Drive or take a bike ride towards Kassiopi. The coastal road is really spectacular, fringed with lush olive trees on one side, jagged rocks jutting into a sparkling sea on the other and the coast of Albania looming in the distance.

Horse riding and walking
Go horse riding along country lanes, through the olive groves, down to Agnos beach. Take a stroll into the hills towards the little Greek villages of Sfakera, Platanos and Nymphes – step back in time along the cobbled alleyways amongst old stone houses or walk along the beach to Almyros, popular with nudists.

TAKING A BREAK

Enigma £–££ Serves Greek, Chinese, Indian, Mexican, British and American specialities, this restaurant caters for all tastes. The children's menu and spacious terrace make it a good choice for families looking for a night out. ⓐ On the main street, just past The Drunken Sailor ① 69761 16246

Odysseus £–££ Menu offers many different starters and good grilled food. ⓐ On the main street ① 26630 63459 ◑ 09.00–23.00

Pangalos £–££ A spit-and-sawdust taverna housed in a quaint old house beside the beach and offering excellent traditional Greek food including fresh seafood, roast meat and steaks. For an exciting dessert, try the

kumquat (a small citrus fruit typical to Corfu) in syrup. ⓐ Roda beach
🕿 69382 88422 🕒 09.00–15.00 & 19.00–23.00

Spiros No 1 £–££ Home-cooked Greek dishes, a spotlessly clean pool, free sunbeds, quiz and bingo nights, pool parties and, best of all, Spiros' potent trio of special cocktails. It's welcoming to children and well worth the short walk out of town. Don't miss the legendary Greek dancing night once a week – for the cost of a reasonably priced set menu, you'll have ringside seats and lots of fun. ⓐ Turn left at the end of the main street 🕿 26630 63429 🕒 12.00–23.00

Harbour ££ Easily recognised by the lighthouse on the roof, this relaxed beach bar has everything from hearty breakfasts, sandwiches and snacks to cocktails and beer served later on in the day. ⓐ Roda beach
🕿 26630 63430 🕒 10.00–02.00

New Port ££ Gentle jazz and a seaview with standard Greek and international fare. ⓐ On the seafront 🕿 26630 63270 🕒 09.00–23.00

Nikos ££ A bustling family-run Greek taverna, the oldest restaurant in Roda, with a simple interior, but excellent food whisked quickly to your table. ⓐ Old Village Road 🕿 26630 63434 🕒 09.30–24.00

Roda Park ££ Traditional Greek cuisine, including *bekhri mezedes*, a mouth-watering combination of pork, ham, cheese and mushrooms cooked in wine sauce and *gioylbassi*, tender chicken baked in a parcel with potatoes. ⓐ Old Village Road 🕿 26630 63212 🆆 www.rodapark.com
🕒 09.00–23.00

AFTER DARK

Crusoes A fun British-run pub with 60s to 80s music, pub food, beer, sports on TV and a range of quizzes throughout the week. ⓐ Main street
🕿 09322 50487 🕒 09.00–17.00

Maggie's A British-run pub attracting a 30-plus crowd to its trivia quizzes, excellent bar meals and a relaxed background of 60s music. Maggie also bakes some mean scones, served with jam and cream, for an indulgent afternoon tea. ⓐ Old village road ❶ 26630 64516 ⏰ 09.00–22.30

Pirates A bar serving English breakfasts and Sunday roast, but turning into a nightlife venue after 17.00 with cocktails, DJs, live music, entertainment and a Greek night every Sunday. ⓐ Seafront ❶ 26630 63394 ⏰ 09.00–04.00

The Drunken Sailor One of the liveliest bars in Roda because of its soundproofing. When Greek law dictates that the music must be turned down, they simply shut the doors and hike up the volume for dancing till dawn. ⓐ Main street ⏰ 22.00–05.00

Roxanne's At 23.00 the action begins in this open-air beer garden, where revellers of all ages dance under the stars. ⓐ Seafront ⏰ 23.00–04.00

Casanova's Hideaway Bar £ Famous loverboy Casanova spent much of 1845 drinking and gambling in Corfu, and this new bar could have been his local, with a good variety of snacks, beer, sports on TV and nightly live entertainment, often by owner and singer Stevie Dell. ⓐ Old village road ⓦ www.steviedell.com ⏰ 12.00–02.00

Mistral £–££ Snacks and film shows during the day, cocktail bar in the evening, full-throttle dance bar by night. Don't miss the Greek dancing, or the quirky donkey racing. ⓐ Main street ❶ 26630 64477 ⏰ 09.00–02.00

Acharavi

Acharavi is set along the main coastal road between Kassiopi and Roda, with hills to one side and a long wide sand-and-pebble beach to the other. A good base for exploring the northern coastline, it's also within reach of the island's highest point – the peak of Mount Pantokrator.

THINGS TO SEE & DO

Hydropolis

The second largest water park in Corfu has three pools, giant slides, a lazy river, a Jacuzzi® and more. Listen to DJ music, play volleyball, basket ball, tennis, water polo or use the internet café.

ⓐ Main road ❶ 26630 64700 ● 09.00–19.00

Mount Pantokrator

Head up to the peak of Mount Pantokrator for spectacular views over Corfu, Albania and the Greek mainland to the east. There's a tiny monastery on the peak (906 m/3,000 ft high).

Old Perithia

Eerie but fascinating, this old village, 700 m (766 yds) up on the slopes of Mount Pantokrator, is almost completely deserted. Entire streets of Venetian houses now stand empty. For centuries, the area was densely populated because its inaccessible position kept the village safe from pirate raids. With the development of the coast, the population of Old Perithia gradually dwindled. Today, there are several friendly tavernas serving drinks and meals to curious tourists.

TAKING A BREAK

Angelos £ Delicious crêpes and other snacks available for eating in or taking out. A good place to end up after a night of barhopping.

ⓐ Main road ❶ 69446 76559 ● 18.00–06.00

Faros £ A family-run cocktail and snack bar overlooking the beach. Enjoy a pizza, crêpe, souvlaki or ice cream in between sunbathing and swimming sessions here. Internet access too. ⓐ Beachfront ⓣ 26630 63214 ⓛ 08.00–03.00 ⓦ www.faroscafe.com

Avra ££ Situated in a beautiful environment, this restaurant offers good-quality food. The chef recommends spaghetti with seafood, lobster and local wine. There is also a playground for children. ⓐ Old village road ⓣ 26630 63633 ⓛ 12.00–23.00

Lemon Garden ££ A large rambling lemon orchard is the exquisite setting for this bar, with drinks by day, barbecue food from 18.00 (120 varieties of gyros!) and cocktails by candlelight and live music later on. The children will love the playground with its car track. ⓐ Main road ⓣ 26630 64446 ⓦ www.lemongarden.gr ⓛ 09.00–02.00

Maestro ££ This large beachside restaurant manages to retain an intimate atmosphere with little oil lamps and gentle Greek music. The fresh fish is especially good. ⓐ Beachfront ⓣ 26630 63020 ⓛ 09.00–23.00

SHOPPING
Atrapos Worth a visit for its unusual bright orange and blue ceramic bowls and jugs, fish platters, bronze candleholders, backgammon sets, silver jewellery and puppets which represent scenes from Greek mythology. ⓣ 26630 64271

Dala's Gold Modern and traditional gold and silver jewellery. ⓣ 06630 63684

Mary's Shop Good ceramics and handmade tablecloths and embroideries at good prices. ⓣ 26630 63425

Elaia Souvenirs made of fragrant carved olive wood, Indonesian handicrafts and jewellery. ⓣ 26630 63425

Le Rustique ££ Traditional Greek taverna with simple furnishings, but excellent Greek specialities with both meat and fish. ⓐ Main road
ⓣ 69447 91834 ⓛ 09.00–23.00

Skondras ££ Lovely, friendly taverna right by the beach with great Greek specialities that many tourists come back for again and again. Try their tasty *meze* for starters. ⓐ Beachfront ⓣ 26630 63048 ⓛ 09.00–23.00

Yanni's ££ A cosy Greek taverna a short walk from the main roundabout, with views over olive groves. Quiet atmosphere with informal service and good food. ⓐ Old village road ⓣ 69777 96230 ⓛ 10.00–23.00

Pumphouse ££–£££ Go Greek with a delicious meatball dish like souzoukakia, take the fish route of fresh lobster and mussels, or choose a delicious selection of *mezedes*. Overlooks the roundabout with the old village water pump. ⓐ Main road ⓣ 26630 63271 ⓛ 12.00–24.00

AFTER DARK

Versus Acharavi's coolest lounge bar has comfortable seating in the garden with views over the street, and a dancefloor in the back. The place really heats up after midnight when DJs play music for a happy crowd. ⓐ Main road ⓣ 26630 63447 ⓛ 17.30–05.00

Yamas £ A cocktail and music bar where the young and lively hang out all day… and night. There's breakfast and snacks in the morning, sports on TV, a DJ spinning discs nightly and happy hours that last all night!
ⓐ Main road ⓛ 07.00–15.30 & 19.00–04.00

Kassiopi

Kassiopi's pretty harbour was once a significant port, and the little village a much-coveted look-out post, attracting the marauding attentions of the Venetians and Turks, among others. Today the only invaders are the tour buses, which fill the harbour square.

THINGS TO SEE & DO

Boat trips

The Travel Corner runs a wide selection of boat tours. You can shop in style by taking an evening cruise from Kassiopi to Corfu Town or enjoy a romantic cruise along the east coast at sunset.
🕐 26630 81220 🖤 www.kassiopi.com

Kassiopitissa Church/Byzantine Fortress

Located behind the Three Brothers restaurant on the harbour, this church dates from 1590 and is said to have been built on the site of a temple of Zeus. Walk up the path opposite the church's bell tower to the ruined Byzantine fortress. It's tangled with bracken and overgrown with wild flowers, but you'll eventually come to a gateway into the fort – follow the walls round to the left for spectacular views over Kassiopi's bay and up to Mount Pantokrator.

TAKING A BREAK

La Luna £–££ Great wines, pizzas, pasta and other Italian dishes served at reasonable prices in a cosy restaurant along Kassiopi's main street. There's outside seating so you can make the most of the evening breeze and the people-watching of course. 🅰 Main street 🕐 26630 82030 🕒 16.00–02.00

Janis ££ A large restaurant with an a la carte menu of Corfiot, Greek, and international meals and several set menus including seafood and vegetarian options. There's a large terrace overlooking Kalamionas beach. Great for that special occasion. ⓐ 100 m (109 yds) from the main square, next to Kalamionas beach ❶ 26630 81082 ❷ 12.00–23.00 May–Sept; closed Oct–Apr ⓦ www.janisrestaurant.com

Petrino ££ A rustic restaurant and wine bar in the village centre serving great Greek and Mediterranean food. The open-air terrace, surrounded by wooden beams, is a cosy place to sit and watch people walk by. ⓐ Kassiopi village, near the main road junction ❶ 26630 81760 ❷ 12.00–01.00

AFTER DARK

Visions A popular bar with over 100 cocktails to choose from to start off your night out. Later on in the evening, the Visions nightclub opens, and English DJs help you party till sunrise. ⓐ Main square ❶ 26630 81974 ⓦ www.visionsbar.com ❷ 10.00–06.00

SHOPPING
Agathi's Lace Shop A wide choice of crisp tablecloths, lace mats, crocheted waistcoats and embroidered napkins.
Aleka's Lace House Exquisite lace and embroidered tablecloths flapping in the breeze on the east of the harbour mark this traditional shop. Lace table-mats are a bargain, and you know it's the real thing as you can see the women at work.
Nikolas Bakery The queue snakes out of the door in the morning as tourists and locals flock to buy *baklava*, chocolate doughnuts, and savoury ham and cheese croissants.

Kalami

A haven on the north-east coast, this horseshoe-shaped bay was once home to author, poet and playright Lawrence Durrell. Tourism has been handled sensitively here and Kalami retains its peaceful fishing village atmosphere.

THINGS TO SEE & DO

Walks

Walk along the footpath, at the back of the White House, to **Yialiskari Bay**, a wonderful spot for swimming, or carry on to **Agni**, an unspoiled pebble bay without a hotel or apartment block in sight.

Watersports

Hire a boat from **Harris Kalami Boats** or learn to water-ski with **Sakis Watersports**.

ⓐ Information on both from the kiosk by the White House Taverna
ⓣ 26630 91646 ⓦ www.corfuboats.gr

TAKING A BREAK

Thomas' Place ££ A great waterfront taverna in the middle of Kalami Bay, set in a century-old fisherman's house. Very popular with Corfu regulars, it serves authentic Greek food and snacks beside the beach.
ⓐ Beachfront ⓣ 26630 91180 ⓛ 09.00–00.30 ⓦ www.thomasplace.gr

Tavernas in Agni

The tiny bay of Agni, just around the headland from Kalami, has been described as the 'gourmet heart of Greece'. Here, on the white-pebble beach, are three exceptional tavernas which are open for lunch and dinner. Free water-taxis run back and forth all evening from Kalami to Agni. It's important to book, and to take the boat marked with the taverna of your choice – otherwise you may end up in one of the others!

Taverna Agni ££–£££ Dating back to 1851, this was built by Eleni's great grandfather. Eleni now creates culinary masterpieces: *mezedes* of succulent sweet peppers, superb courgette fritters and the plumpest of mussels, followed by wild mountain beef. ⓐ Agni beach ⓣ 26630 91142 ⓛ 07.30–23.00 ⓦ www.agni.gr/taverna_agni/taverna_agni.asp

Taverna Nikolas ££–£££ Genuine Corfiot village food whose flavours are rarely found outside a Greek home. *Arni lemonato* (lamb with lemons) is mouth-wateringly succulent. ⓐ Agni beach ⓣ 26630 91136 ⓛ 08.00–23.00 ⓦ www.agnibay.com

Toula's Taverna ££–£££ Specialises in seafood – such as grilled sea bream or lobster. The prawn pilaff is legendary, cooked to order while you sample the delicious appetisers. ⓐ Agni beach ⓣ 26630 91503 ⓛ 07.30–23.00

AFTER DARK

Kalami Cocktail Bar Wind up the evening at this cosy first-floor bar with views over the village road. Golden oldies with a few 80s and 90s hits thrown in make for a mellow evening. ⓐ Main street ⓣ 26630 91579 ⓛ 18.00–01.00

ⓐ *Kalami offers a peaceful atmosphere*

Nissaki

The sleepy atmosphere of this little village makes relaxation as easy as ordering your first chilled beer. No noisy discos to disturb the peace, just a sprinkling of restaurants and local shops.

BEACHES

Nissaki Bay has the smallest of the three beaches, a tiny white-pebbled cove nestling at the bottom of a steep hill. At **Kaminaki beach**, the crystal-clear water is a snorkeller's paradise. Go down the steep hill, or through the olive groves from the main road. **Krouseri** has a long pebbly beach with watersports facilities, boat trips and sunbeds.

TAKING A BREAK

Anthi Taverna ££ People-watch from the vine-covered terrace, which looks out over the sparkling turquoise sea. ⓐ Main street, north of the church ⓣ 26630 91069 ⓛ 09.00–23.00

Mitsos ££ A traditional Greek family taverna perched on a rock in the sea with unrivalled views. ⓐ Nissaki Bay ⓣ 26630 91240 ⓦ www.mitsostaverna.gr ⓛ 09.00–23.00

Olive Press ££ Set in olive groves above the bay, you can sample excellent Greek dishes in a romantic atmosphere. ⓐ Nissaki Road ⓣ 26630 91698 ⓛ 10.00–24.00

Parea ££ The tavern of choice in Nissaki is set just behind a small pebble beach, and serves authentic fresh Greek food, fresh fish, and lots of *meze* options at affordable prices. There's also pasta and pizza with a local twist. ⓐ Nissaki beach ⓣ 26630 91359 ⓦ www.corfu-nissaki-parea.eu ⓛ 10.00–24.00

● *Nissaki is the perfect place to relax and sunbathe*

Vitamins ££ Dimitris and his family run this friendly restaurant named after the consistently good and healthy food served here for over 30 years. Book ahead for a seaview table on the lovely terrace overlooking the bay. ⓐ Main road, towards Corfu Town ① 26630 91278 ⓦ www.vitaminstaverna.com ⓛ 10.00–24.00

Dimitris £££ With fabulous views over Kalami, this is the place for that special occasion. Souvlaki, lobster and oyster mushrooms are all on the menu. ⓐ Main road, towards Kassiopi ① 26630 91172 ⓛ 19.00–24.00

SHOPPING

Supermarket Afrodite A large selection of fresh food and groceries, plus a wonderful bakery next door. ⓐ On the main coastal road about 100 m (109 yds) after the church

Symposium A fabulous store of local foods and wines, and fresh rolls and croissants. ⓐ A few hundred metres south of Supermarket Afrodite ① 26630 91094

Barbati

Known as the 'Riviera', this part of the north-east coast of Corfu has silvery olive groves growing to the sea, separated from it only by a wide strip of shingle, with the rocky flanks of Mount Pantokrator standing majestically as a backdrop. The beach is sheltered and offers safe bathing, making it very popular with families.

THINGS TO DO

Watersports
Barbati Ski Club Parasailing, waterskiing and other activities all available on the beach.
ⓐ In front of Akti Barbati bar and restaurant ❶ 26630 91230

Boat trips with Vivi
Pedaloes for hire and boat trips in a caique to Agni, Aghios Stefanos, Corfu Town, Vidos, Mouse Island, etc.
❶ Call Yakkis on 6932 452739 (mobile) or drop in to Taverna Glyfa to see his brother Nikolas (see page 73) ❶ Ask your rep for more details

TAKING A BREAK

Akti £–££ Smart lavender-blue and white is the theme on this terrace overlooking the beach, shaded by lovely old olive and oleander trees. Breakfasts, snacks, *mezedes* and Corfiot specialities such as *pastitsada* (see page 97). ⓐ Barbati beach ❶ 26630 91276 ❶ 12.00–19.00

Anthi ££ A terrace overlooks the sea at this very pleasant spot serving delicious ice creams, pizzas and fresh fish and much else besides.
ⓐ Main street, opposite Lord Byron ❶ 09.00–23.00

Lord Byron ££ The oldest taverna in Barbati contains a treasure trove of flags from all over the world displayed behind the bar. The menu includes everything from fish fingers to lobster. This is a lively spot, especially in the evenings. ⓐ Main street, towards Nissaki ⓣ 26630 91577 ⓛ 09.00–23.00

Taverna Glyfa ££ Two terraces overlook the sparkling sea and little coves in this romantic setting. Delicious peppered steaks, sea bass, local fresh fish and lobster in season are all on the menu. Greek dancing nights and live music every week. ⓐ Main road, towards Nissaki ⓣ 26630 91317 ⓛ 09.00–01.00

AFTER DARK

Jasos £ A small café-bar popular with an older crowd. Great for winding down with a beer or cocktail after a day on the beach. ⓐ Main road, towards Nissaki ⓛ 17.00–24.00

Agathi £–££ A cocktail bar with superb views of the sea and Corfu Town in the distance from the terrace bar. Try ice creams, snacks, cocktails or any other kind of drink. ⓐ Main road, towards Ipsos ⓣ 26630 91445 ⓛ 10.00–24.00

SHOPPING
The nearest **bakery** is just down the road at Nissaki on the main coastal road next to **Supermarket Afrodite**. Also, Aphrodite at the **Laundry Express Service** will wash, dry, iron and deliver your laundry for a very reasonable price. There's also a dry-cleaning service. ⓣ 26630 91590 ⓛ 09.00–19.00 Mon–Sat, 09.30–14.30 Sun

Ipsos

Ipsos sits on the shore of a long shingle bay which is known as the 'Golden Mile'. During the day, the beach and watersports claim the attention of most holidaymakers. By night the resort sings out into the early hours.

BEACHES

Ipsos beach runs parallel to the main road in a narrow strip of shingle. A few kilometres further north, **Barbati** offers an unspoiled, white-pebble beach surrounded by lush mountain scenery. If you're planning to beach-hop, the Ipsos–Kassiopi road is a beautiful drive as well as taking you past **Kaminaki**, **Kalami**, **Agni** and the picturesque harbour of **Kouloura**.

THINGS TO SEE & DO

Aghios Markos

A left-hand fork just after Pyrgi takes you to Aghios Markos on a pretty 2-km (1½-mile) stroll into rural Corfu, along a lemon-tree-studded road, past orange orchards, wild carnations and dilapidated farm buildings. The tiny half-ruined Monastery of Christ Pantokrator sits on the hillside over the village and affords a lovely view over the countryside below. Stop for some 'moon juice' (the potent local beer) or a simple lunch at the Panorama bar.

Boat trips

Captain Homer runs several boat excursions, including one to Kassiopi with swimming stops on the way back, and to Benitses, Mouse Island and Vidos in the south. Both include generous amounts of barbecue food and drink.

ⓐ Ipsos harbour ① 26610 97426

Diving
Try scuba diving or do a full course at Waterhopper.
ⓐ Opposite Dino's ⓣ 26610 93867 ⓛ 09.00–13.00 and 18.00–21.00, closed Sun

Go-karting
Bounce off tyre barriers and tackle hairpin bends down at the go-kart track, which is set back 50 m (54 yds) from the main coastal road, next to B52.

Horse riding
Get off the beaten track and explore rural Corfu on horseback. **The Rider's Club**, organises rides on good horses for all levels of experience from novice to old hand.
ⓐ Korakiana village ⓣ 26630 22503

Mount Pantokrator
Hire a car and drive through the olive groves to Spartilas, at the foot of Mount Pantokrator, continuing up to Strinilas, perched on the mountainside. Hike to the peak for fantastic views, then descend through a densely wooded valley via Eriva, Lafki and down to Acharavi. The picturesque drive through the multi-hued trees and flowers is very peaceful, with hardly a car or house in sight.

SHOPPING

Moons A Greek-style homeware department store, with wooden hand-painted clocks, scented candles, rugs, cushions, night lights and glassware. The ceramics are bright and attractive and there's also a trendy selection of dresses, shoes and stylish silver jewellery.
ⓐ Main road going towards Dassia

Tina's Jewellery Another place to shop for beautiful silver bracelets and bangles, swish watches and sparkling rings.
ⓐ Main road going towards Dassia

TAKING A BREAK

Unless otherwise stated, all the following restaurants are on the main road going towards Pyrgi.

Calypso £ A quiet café-restaurant with a nice garden terrace, and a modern interior, serving snacks, great ice cream and cakes.
🕓 09.00–03.00

Pizzeria Bonita £ Attention to detail makes dining on this candlelit terrace a real pleasure. Wonderful pizzas and rich pasta dishes at low prices. ❸ Pirgi, just above Ipsos ❶ 26610 93293 🕓 12.00–23.00

Phoebus £–££ Very good and reasonably priced Greek food on a terrace overlooking the beach – you'll be hard pressed to find better *kleftiko* or *stifado* elsewhere. ❶ 26610 93386 🕓 18.00–24.00

Little Italy ££ The romantic garden setting amongst pots, palm trees and hammocks is perhaps the prettiest dinner spot in Ipsos. Generous-sized portions of pasta and wood oven pizzas. Save room for the *tiramisu*.
❶ 26610 97720 🕓 10.00–23.00

The Viceroy ££ Spice up your holiday with a vindaloo, chicken tikka or biryani in this nicely decorated Indian restaurant – the first one in Corfu.
❶ 26610 93814 🕓 19.00–24.00, closed Mon

Peking House ££–£££ Smarter than most of the restaurants along the main drag, this is one of the better Chinese restaurants in Corfu, serving a range of delicious Cantonese and Szechuan cuisine. ❶ 26610 93646
🕓 12.00–23.00

AFTER DARK

All the following venues are on the main road.

Bambooza Enjoy a quiet(ish) cocktail on the upstairs balcony with a view over the sea or head inside to the disco for some groovy, up-to-date sounds and the latest dance music. Popular with early 20s and tour groups.
🕐 12.00–01.00

B52 See and be seen in this sophisticated cocktail bar. Pool tables, screens and good drinks amuse a 20–30s crowd till the early morning.
🕐 17.00–04.00

Dinos Less rowdy than the younger bars along the front, there's still a great atmosphere here. It's a favourite with anyone whose knowledge of pop music runs out after about 1986, and with couples looking for a fun evening out which can also accommodate a toddler or two. Serves value-for-money Greek and English food. ⓐ Past Temple Bar
ⓕ 26610 97517 🕐 10.00–01.00

🔺 *The coastline near Ipsos is known as the 'Golden Mile'*

Dirty Nellies In one of the liveliest spots, a young 20s crowd chatters, dances and drinks with Irish hosts Ursula and Theo. Karaoke and all kinds of games, which can get very boisterous indeed. ☎ 26610 93615
🕒 10.00–03.00

Hector's The most popular club in Ipsos, with people of all ages partying till dawn to a medley of music. Loud music, foreign DJs, drinks and lots of dancing. ☎ 26630 93014 🕒 22.30–07.00

Jupiter A popular, loud club playing house music to ecstatic crowds until sunrise. 📍 Next to Montechristo 🕒 01.00–07.00

Montechristo A popular club on the middle of the strip, with legendary foam parties – you'll be up to your shoulders in the white stuff.
🕒 23.00–05.00

Old Tree A lively bar where you can drink, dance, or just hang out, all day and all night too. 🕒 10.00–03.00

Shooters A mad bar full of youngsters trying to have as much fun and drinks as possible – with hilarious effects. 📍 Next to Old Tree
🕒 17.00–03.00

Temple Bar In the early evening English food is served on the terrace overlooking the sea. Later on in the evening, in the bar on the other side of the road, there's entertainment, karaoke, pole dancing by 'volunteers' plucked from the audience, and dancing to the sounds of the 70s and 80s.
📍 Northern end 🌐 www.corfutemple.com 🕒 11.00–03.00

Dassia

Dassia's curving bay, fringed by a long stretch of silver shingle, is home to some of the best watersports on the island. Days in Dassia are spent water-skiing, windsurfing, parascending or racing through the water. In the evening the action moves to the main road, which is lined with restaurants, bars and shops. Terraces hum with chatter and gentle music, plates smash and crash in displays of Greek dancing, and cocktails are shaken, stirred and replenished. Many of the restaurants combine quality food with entertainment and the resort is lively until midnight and beyond.

THINGS TO SEE & DO

Boat trips
Spend a leisurely day cruising past Nissaki, Kalami and Kouloura to Kassiopi for a spot of shopping or sightseeing, or head south to Benitses past Corfu Town. Check which boat trips are on offer at the jetties along the beach.

Cycling
Rent a bike from **The Corfu Mountainbike Shop**, near the Elea Beach Hotel, and explore the area. They also run several escorted tours for all levels of fitness through picturesque villages and along country lanes and donkey tracks.
🕿 26610 93344 🖤 www.mountainbikecorfu.gr 🕒 Mar–Oct

Paintballing
There's no better thing in the world than shooting paint capsules at your friends, and here's the place to do it in the centre of Dassia.
🅐 Main road 🕿 26610 97990 🕒 10.00–22.00

TAKING A BREAK

Great Shakes £–££ Kick-start the day in this cosy British-run bar with the massive cooked breakfast. A daytime snack menu of chip butties and

omelettes gives way to more substantial family favourites (cod and chips, cottage pie) in the evening. Shakes organises regular quiz nights too. ⓐ Main road ⓣ 26610 93789 ⓦ www.greatshakescorfu.com
ⓛ 09.00–01.00

Vinieri ££ A lovely art and food café, and set back from the bustle of the resort. ⓐ Dassia–Katomeri Road, past the Victoria Hotel ⓣ 26610 93980
ⓛ 10.00–14.00 & 18.00–24.00

Walnut Tree (Karydia) ££ A traditional taverna with terrace serving delicious Corfiot and Greek specialities, including a tasty roast goat. Very popular. ⓐ Main road ⓣ 26610 93432 ⓛ 10.00–24.00

Dionysos ££–£££ Low lighting, low music but high quality, this classy taverna offers excellent meat dishes at tables set between stone arches and pots of flowers. Leave room for the liqueur-laced desserts – they're delicious. ⓐ Main road ⓣ 26610 93449 ⓛ 18.00–01.00

Etrusco £££ Excellent international restaurant with a strong Italian flavour, perfect for a special occasion. It is well worth the effort to discover this hidden treasure. The turn-off is up the hill near to Sophia's corner, from where it is signposted. Reservations necessary.
ⓐ Between Dassia and Ipsos ⓣ 26610 93342 ⓛ 20.00–01.00

AFTER DARK

Edem Bar A very popular beach bar with a lovely natural stone and wood interior. Foreign DJs often play here, with music varying from house to disco. ⓐ Dassia beach ⓣ 26610 93013 ⓛ 09.00–04.00
ⓦ www.edemclub.com

Woodpecker Pub £ A spacious garden terrace pub with a wide range of cocktails, beers and snacks. ⓐ Main road ⓣ 26610 93797
ⓛ 19.00–03.00

Kontokali & Gouvia

The building of a new marina at Kontokali a few years ago transformed this quiet village into a busy holiday resort. It has now become a popular playground for the Greeks, as well as for British, American and German tourists, and is ideally placed for trips to Corfu Town and around the north of the island.

BEACHES

Kontokali sits in its own little bay of fine sand and pebbles and very clean water. Cleared of weed and debris at the crack of dawn every morning, it's a Blue Flag beach with sunbeds and umbrellas for hire. The pebble beach of Gouvia lies just further north, with a view of the whitewashed church of Ipapanti opposite.

THINGS TO SEE & DO

Ipapanti Church

Visit the Ipapanti church in its picturesque setting at the end of a narrow causeway jutting out into Gouvia bay. Reached by the road to Kommeno, it was built under Venetian rule in 1713 by the son of a Cretan aristocrat and restored to its former glory in 1996. Look out for the two festivals celebrated at the Ipapanti church – its own feast day, on 2 February, and Aghia Marina, on 17 July.

Lagoon

For a small entrance fee, a great pool and excellent facilities for children await you here. Poolside bar, crazy golf and five-a-side football too – if you have the energy.

ⓐ Gouvia ❶ 26610 80091 ⏲ 10.00–18.00

TAKING A BREAK

Gorgona ££ Not cheap, but you're paying for the excellent fresh fish and seafood, and other imaginative dishes. ⓐ Main road, Gouvia ⓣ 26610 90261 ⓛ 12.00–24.00

Koh Samui ££ The first Thai restaurant on Corfu (newly opened in 2007), this small restaurant has a great variety of mild to fiery dishes, including *padthai gai* (noodles with chicken and egg) and curries. Wash it all down with a Singha beer. Free delivery to hotels in the area. ⓐ Main road, Gouvia ⓣ 26610 99163 ⓛ 18.00–01.30

Molfatta ££ An excellent restaurant and bar near the beach, with dimmed lights hung in baskets, soft music and Greek dancing on weekend nights. Great for a romantic dinner. ⓐ Gouvia beach ⓣ 26610 91915 ⓛ 09.00–02.00

9 Muses ££ Homemade Greek specialities and a variety of steaks with international and spicy sauces. ⓐ Main road, Gouvia ⓣ 26610 99163 ⓛ 18.00–01.30

O Makis ££ If it lives in the sea, you'll find it here – grilled, sprinkled with herbs and served with a twist of lemon. Delicious red mullet, red snapper, king prawns and grilled lobster. ⓐ Main road, Kontokali ⓣ 26610 91814 ⓛ 12.00–23.00

Papilias Taverna ££ An authentic local taverna overlooking the main crossroads in town. Good Greek *mezes* and dinners, and tasty fresh fish meals. ⓐ Main road, Kontokali ⓣ 26610 91201 ⓛ 10.00–23.00

Zorba's Taverna ££ Geraniums and a palm tree growing through the wooden verandah make this a pleasant, shady spot for everything from English breakfast and hamburgers to Corfiot specialities and good

grilled fish. Greek dancing weekly. ⓐ Kontokali ❶ 26610 90184
🕒 08.00–23.00

Roula ££–£££ Situated on a small island overlooking Gouvia Marina, you
may need to book for this superb seafood place. ⓐ Gerekos island,
Kontokali ❶ 26610 91382 🕒 12.00–24.00

Argo £££ Overlooking the marina in Gouvia, where snazzy yachts jostle
for moorings, the Argo is modern, clean and classy with a sophisticated
menu and a good – if expensive – selection of wines. ⓐ Gouvia Marina
❶ 26610 99251 🕒 09.00–23.00

Gerekos £££ A fish feast fit for kings, or at least for the international
celebrities who frequent this quaint, intimate restaurant. It's one of the
best fish tavernas on the island and well worth a splurge. ⓐ Main road,
Kontokali ❶ 26610 91281 🕒 12.00–23.00

🔺 *Kontokali: popular playground*

AFTER DARK

Beer Bucket The perfect spot for Men Behaving Badly – it's draught beer, laddishness and dancing on the bar. With live rhythm and blues bands once a week, this fun pub lets the good times roll. ⓐ Main road, Kontokali ① 26610 90750 Ⓦ www.beerbucketcorfu.com ① 09.00–02.00

G & M Very friendly, lively bar. Dance to the sounds of music played by Greek DJs or just sit outside and relax drinking your favourite cocktail. ⓐ Main street, Kontokali ① 16.00–02.00

Melodies A modern pub with a twinkling starry ceiling, great staff and music set at a level that you can hear others too. ⓐ Main road, Gouvia ① 26610 90606 ① 18.00–02.00

Status A rocking club popular with night owls from as far as Corfu Town. ⓐ Main road, Gouvia, near Whispers and the roundabout ① 24.00–06.00

Whispers A wide mix of fun-lovers frequents this popular venue – mostly young and gorgeous, so you'll fit right in! ⓐ Main road, Gouvia ① 24.00–06.00

● *Parga's Valtos beach*

Achilleion Palace

Used as the location for the James Bond film *For Your Eyes Only* (1981), this neoclassical palace – with its impressive gardens and lavish interior – is an interesting detour through a fragment of Corfu's history.

The elaborate villa was commissioned in 1889 by Elizabeth, Empress of Austria, who instructed two Italian architects to design a palace 'worthy of Achilles', her favourite hero from ancient Greek literature. It was completed two years later and she used it until her death in 1898 as an escape from the Hapsburg court and her domineering mother-in-law.

THINGS TO SEE & DO

The palace

The ground floor of the palace is open to visitors. You'll see cherubs hanging from every wall, Corinthian pillars springing up in the stairwells, and gilded mirrors reflecting fancy decorations. The reception hall has a frescoed ceiling by the Italian painter Galopi, depicting the four seasons. There are also mementoes of Kaiser Wilhelm, including the desk where he used to plan his strategies for World War I. The palace was used as a hospital during World Wars I and II and the Grand Casino was housed on the second floor until 1992.

The gardens

The gardens are beautifully maintained, filled with palm trees and wonderful flowers as well as some notable statues. You can't miss Victorious Achilles, a huge statue weighing 4.5 tonnes and standing over 11 m (36 ft) tall. It was the brainchild of Kaiser Wilhelm II who wanted to reflect his own power in Achilles' imposing stance. The Empress Elizabeth commissioned the Dying Achilles from the German sculptor Ernst Herter in 1884. It depicts Achilles attempting to pull the poisoned arrow from his only weak spot, his right heel.

The Muses colonnade, forming the upper terrace, is decorated with statues of the nine Muses and the three Graces. The first statue in the far left-hand corner, next to Venus, is Apollo holding a lyre, the work of Italian sculptor Canova. Peer through the wrought-iron door under the colonnade to see the palace's most valuable painting, the enormous The Triumph of Achilles by the Austrian painter, Franz Matsch.

Practicalities

Achilleion Palace ⓐ 8 km (5 miles) south of Corfu Town ⓘ 26610 56210 ⓛ 08.00–19.00 ⓘ Admission charge. The palace is extremely busy in the late morning and early afternoon so, if you can, get there when it opens or in the late afternoon.

⬧ Achilleion Palace terrace

Albania

Just 2 km (1 mile) from Corfu at the nearest point, Albania was for a long time the most isolated and paranoid dictatorship in Europe. The country is now recovering fast, and is rapidly developing its tourism facilities. The southern harbour town of Saranda and the nearby ancient ruins at Butrint can easily be visited on a short trip from Corfu Town.

Saranda

The harbour town of Saranda is a modern but pleasant place to start exploring this little-known country. After arrival and passport checks at the fancy customs building, it's just a short walk south past the open-air market place to the town centre. There are some decent restaurants (try Albanian food which is a delicious mix of Greek and Turkish) and various shops with Albanian T-shirts and souvenirs along the seafront. One block back from the harbour is the main square with a small ongoing excavation.

Butrint

The archaeological site and national park at Butrint, 24 km (15 miles) south of Saranda, is one of Albania's highlights and is not to be missed. The drive there over smooth new roads gives you a glimpse of Albania's beautiful countryside. Watch out for the small bunkers which dictator Enver Hoxha put up everywhere.

Butrint has been inhabited since prehistoric times, and what you see now was mainly left by Illyrians, Greeks, Romans, Byzantines, and Ottomans. Excavations started under Italian rule, and have been picked up in the 1990s by a British-run foundation. Unlike many Greek excavations, Butrint is still mainly covered with vegetation, making for a lovely shaded walk (but bring mosquito repellent). The remains include a theatre which could hold up to 2,500 people, an early Christian church with some lovely mosaics (often kept covered to preserve them), the remains of a temple, a baptistry and the massive stone Lion Gate. The Akropolis on top of the hill offers great views over the site and the lake and hills around. Nature enthusiasts should take time to walk along the marked paths in the surrounding national park, which teems with bird life.

Practicalities

Several tourist boats depart daily for day trips to Albania; the crossing lasts 75 minutes and tickets can be booked at any travel agent. **Ionian Cruises** (ⓐ New harbour, Corfu Town ① 26610 38690 ⓦ www.ioniancruises.com) runs services including a hydrofoil (taking 25 minutes), departing Corfu Town daily at 09.00, with return trips at 13.00 (daily except Monday) and 16.15. You can book tickets through agents but it's cheaper to book online.

EU citizens and most Westerners do not need a visa for Albania, but do need to pay a €10 entrance fee if planning to stay for more than a day. Albania's currency is the Lek (£1 = 172 Lek, $1 = 83 Lek, 1 euro € = 121 Lek as of November 2007), and is easily available at exchange offices and reliable ATMs (cash machines) along the waterfront in Saranda. Local restaurants will also accept euros for payment, though the exchange rate won't be great.

● *The archaeological site at Butrint is popular with tourists*

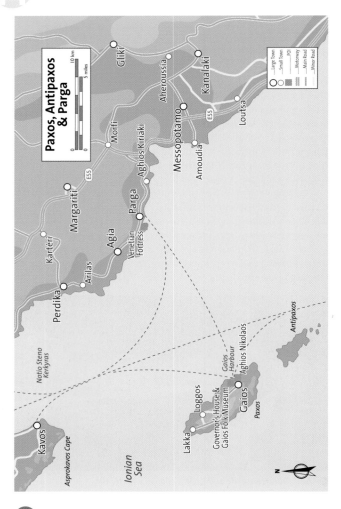

Paxos, Antipaxos & Parga

Parga

The attractive, terracotta-roofed town of Parga huddles amongst olive groves on the Greek mainland overlooking its sheltered harbour. Pastel-coloured and whitewashed houses with floral balconies line narrow alleyways, threading up into the hills behind the port. An old fort stands guard at the western end of the bay, with a tiny islet and church sitting prettily in the middle.

BEACHES

Relax in the sun on the sand-and-shingle Krioneri beach which, despite its location near the ferry boats, has clean, clear water. Enjoy the view of the islet opposite, or hire a pedalo and paddle round it. Sandy Valtos beach, just a short walk away over the headland beyond the fortress, is larger but also more exposed to the afternoon wind.

▲ *Parga is an attractive town on the Greek mainland*

THINGS TO SEE & DO

Parga Castle

Walk up to the old Venetian-era castle for a bird's-eye view over the bay.
It is crumbling and overgrown, cannon barrels lie higgledy-piggledy on
the grass, butterflies dance against the blue sky and the higher levels are
shaded with fir trees – ideal for a lunchtime picnic or visit to the café
(see below). The far side of the castle offers a wonderful panorama over
Valtos beach and the craggy mountain beyond, but hold on to the
children as there are few safety barriers.

🕐 09.00–21.00

TAKING A BREAK

Café inside the Castle £ Sit in the shade of fragrant pine trees with
beautiful views over town while sipping coffee. ⓐ Parga Castle
🕐 26840 31150 🕑 09.30–02.00 Ⓦ www.pargaweb.com/castle-cafe

Eden £ An American-run bistro serving pasta, ice cream, healthy
sandwiches, homemade cakes and both sweet and savoury crêpes.
ⓐ 26 Vassila St 🕐 26840 31409 🕑 10.00–01.00

Dionysos ££ One of the oldest tavernas in town, serving up good
portions of delicious fresh fish and other Greek specialities. ⓐ Corner of
the harbourfront and Krioneri beach 🕐 69451 43793 🕑 09.00–24.00

Paxos

Only 11 km (7 miles) in length, Paxos is the smallest and perhaps most upmarket of the main Ionian islands. There's a very relaxed feel about the place, and the islanders are said to be the friendliest in Greece. There are three natural harbours; ferries arrive at the most southerly, Gaios, also the island's capital, which is protected by two little islets – the tiny Panayia, and the pine-clad islet of Aghios Nikolaos.

Paxos is a mass of silvery-green olive trees with dramatic limestone cliffs to the west. Boats from the harbour make regular trips past the tiny sister island of Antipaxos, and into the sea caves, where the sun reflecting off the pale rocks gives the water a bright, almost luminous, blue sheen. Combined day trips to Paxos and Parga usually also take in the eastern coast of Corfu, a wonderful way to see Corfu Town and its fortresses from the sea. Keep your eyes peeled, as you might see dolphins playing in the water if you're lucky.

To find out more about cruises, visit Ⓦ www.ioniancruises.com/cruise_parga_paxos.htm

THINGS TO SEE & DO

Gaios

Gaios harbour is a picturesque mish-mash of shops, tavernas and cafés where you can sit and enjoy the view. Along the southern harbourfront is the **Governor's House**, used by the Venetians and later the British. This lovely building has a faded charm and currently houses the historical and folk collection of the Paxos Museum.

ⓘ 11.30–14.30 & 19.30–23.30 ❶ Admission charge

Behind the harbour is a web of pretty streets and walking south along the road parallel to the harbour, you will pass through olive groves. There are several little beaches along the coast with wonderfully clear water – excellent for snorkelling.

Lakka and Loggos

Some boat cruises stop off at one of Paxos' other settlements, Lakka and Loggos – both very pretty villages nestled in small harbours, offering good-quality tavernas.

TAKING A BREAK

Anneta ££ A popular eatery along Gaios' waterfront, with great views of the bustle of the harbour. Excellent fish and grilled meat in oil from the island. ⓐ Gaios, waterfront ⓣ 26620 32670 ⓛ 09.30–23.00

Olive Tree ££–£££ Signposted from the harbour, this tiny taverna has romantic tables set in an attractive alley. The imaginative menu lists fresh fish, Greek and Mediterranean dishes. ⓐ Loggos ⓣ 69728 52043 ⓛ 11.30–24.00

La Rosa di Paxos £££ Upmarket dining on a flower-filled terrace on the waterfront. Italian specialities, fish and a fine collection of wines. ⓐ Lakka, waterfront ⓣ 26620 31471 ⓛ 12.00–23.00

◗ *Greek orthodox priests in Corfu town*

Food & drink

Corfu's restaurants cater for an international palate, with steak, pizza and pasta featuring heavily on many menus. The larger resorts also have a fair sprinkling of English, Italian, Indian and Chinese eateries. Traditional Greek – and Corfiot – dishes are available everywhere, and the holidaymaker who steps beyond the familiar moussaka, feta cheese and taramasalata will be richly rewarded.

STARTERS

The traditional start to any Greek meal is *mezedes* – a selection of appetisers – accompanied by a glass of *ouzo*. Typical offerings will be *kalamarakia tiganita* (fried squid), *dolmadákia* (vine leaves stuffed with rice, onions and currants), *melitzanosalata* (puréed aubergines flavoured with garlic, onion, tomato and lemon juice), *taramosalata* (cod's roe dip), *skordalia* (a thick, creamy garlic dip), and *tzatziki* (a garlicky cucumber and yoghurt dip).

Hot choices are cheese *saganaki* (deep-fried chunks of regato or Kefalotiri goat's cheese), *spanakopitta* (a flaky filo pastry spinach pie), or *keftedakia* (mini meatballs). *Fasoladha* is a rich tomato, olive oil and haricot bean soup.

MAIN COURSES

Unsurprisingly, all kinds of fish are on the Corfiot menu. The menu will often just say 'fish' and the waiter will tell you which delights landed in that day's catch. *Barbouni* (red mullet), *lithrini* (sea bream) and many others are at their best simply grilled over charcoal.

Lobster is good and nowhere near as expensive as back home (it is usually priced by the kilo on menus, so check the total cost before you order). King prawns are often served as kebabs and a tasty dish for fish lovers is shrimp *saganaki* – shrimps baked in cheese and tomato sauce. *Midia yemista* (stuffed mussels baked in their shells) and *oktapodi skordato* (octopus marinated in red wine and herbs) are other delicious choices.

Meat in Corfu is tender and plentiful. There are several specialities peculiar to the island that you will find on every menu, from the simplest rural taverna to the swankiest hotel dining room. Wherever you are, be sure to try them. *Pastitsada* is traditionally cockerel meat or beef in a tomato sauce served on a bed of spaghetti, rice or potatoes. Escalopes of veal or beef, covered in a garlic wine sauce, is the basis for *sofrito*. *Stifado* is beef stewed in a slightly spicy tomato and olive oil sauce with lots of baby onions. *Kokinisto* (chunks of beef in red wine) also makes a popular dish. Lamb lovers will relish the spit roast, which often accompanies

⬤ *A delectable spread of typical Greek dishes*

celebrations for saints' days, or *kleftiko* – lamb baked in a parcel of tin foil with garlic and vegetables. Simple *souvlaki* – chargrilled pork or chicken on a skewer – is a delight, usually served with rice and salad. The word *gyros* usually signifies a fast-food option of meat from a revolving spit served in pitta.

Vegetarianism is still quite a novel concept, although some of the more enlightened restaurants have a special menu. There's a reasonable amount of choice, with dishes such as *papoutsakia* – aubergines stuffed with herbs and vegetables – or *domates yemistes nistisimes* – tomatoes filled with rice, mint, onions and feta, with some places also serving meat-free *moussaka*. *Briam*, a tomato-based casserole of potatoes, courgettes, onions and green beans, and *prassopitta*, layered filo pastry filled with leeks, are tasty alternatives.

◆ *Ouzo – a traditional accompaniment to any meal*

DESSERTS

Fruit is the traditional end to a Greek meal. However, for the sweet-toothed, satisfaction can be gained from the many variations of the wickedly sweet *baklava* – filo pastry stuffed with nuts and dipped in honey. Sorbets and ice creams are another popular finish to a meal, as is thick, creamy yoghurt with honey and, sometimes, nuts. Cheesecake, chocolate cake, apple pie and other standard international desserts are available in many tourist areas, albeit with a Greek twist.

DRINKS

Mezedes are traditionally accompanied by a glass of aniseed-flavoured *ouzo* which is served with chilled water. Beer drinkers will usually be offered Amstel, although the Greek lagers Mythos and Alpha are also popular. In bars geared towards the English market, beers like Newcastle Brown, Boddingtons and Caffreys are widely available.

Many restaurants serve local wine from the barrel, which is often surprisingly good. Apelia and Boutari are inexpensive, reasonable whites, with Tsantali turning up the quality a notch or two. Patras is a decent dry white. Good red wines are Boutari Grand Reserve, Calliga Rubis and the full-bodied Nemea.

Retsina, pine-resin-flavoured white wine, is an acquired taste. Served chilled, it's very refreshing and may well grow on you.

All the usual soft drinks – Coke, Fanta and Sprite – are sold everywhere. Ask for soda if you want sparkling mineral water. Greek coffee is served in tiny cups, complete with the grounds – so don't drain your cup. Ask for 'Nescafé' if you want something akin to coffee back home.

Expect to pay a cover charge in restaurants, which usually includes bread. Service is usually included in your bill, but it is common also to leave a tip for the waiter, or to round up the bill.

Menu decoder

Here are some of the authentic Greek dishes that you might encounter in tavernas or pastry shops.

Dolmadákia Vine leaves stuffed with rice, onions, currants, dill, parsley, mint and lemon juice

Domátes/piperiés yemistés Tomatoes/peppers stuffed with herb-flavoured rice (and sometimes minced lamb or beef)

Fassólia saláta White beans (haricot, butter beans) dressed with olive oil, lemon juice, parsley, onions, olives and tomato

Lazánia sto fourno Greek lasagne, similar to Italian lasagne, but often including additional ingredients, such as chopped boiled egg or sliced, Greek-style sausages

Makaronópita A pie made from macaroni blended with beaten eggs, cheese and milk, baked in puff pastry

Melitzanópita A pie made from baked liquidised aubergines mixed with onions, garlic, breadcrumbs, eggs, mint and parmesan cheese

Melitzano saláta Aubergine dip made from baked aubergines, liquidised with tomatoes, onions and lemon juice

Mezedes A selection of appetisers, such as **tzatziki, dolmadákia** and **melitzano saláta**

Moussakás Moussaka, made from fried slices of aubergines, interlayered with minced beef and **béchamel** sauce

Pastítsio Layers of macaroni, parmesan cheese and minced meat (cooked with onions, tomatoes and basil), topped with **béchamel** sauce and baked

Píta me kymá Meat pie made from minced lamb and eggs, flavoured with onions and cinnamon and baked in filo pastry

Saláta horiátiki Country salad (known in England as 'Greek salad'); every restaurant has its own recipe, but the basic ingredients are tomatoes, cucumber, onions, green peppers, black olives and feta cheese, dressed with vinegar, olive oil and oregano

Souvláki Kebab – usually of pork – cooked over charcoal

Spanakotyropitákia Cigar-shaped pies made from feta cheese, eggs, spinach, onions and nutmeg in filo pastry

Taramosaláta Cod's roe dip made from puréed potatoes, smoked cod's roe, oil, lemon juice and onion

Tyropitákia Small triangular cheese pies made from feta cheese and eggs in filo pastry

Tzatzíki Grated cucumber and garlic in a dressing of yoghurt, olive oil and vinegar

THE KAFENEION

In Greek villages, the **kafeneion** (café) remains very much a male preserve, although visitors of both sexes will be made welcome. Customers come to read the paper, debate the issues of the day and play backgammon, as well as to consume **elinikos kafés** (Greek coffee). This is made by boiling finely ground beans in a special pot with a long handle. Sugar is added during the preparation rather than at the table, so you should order **glyko** (sweet), **metrio** (medium) or **sketo** (no sugar). In summer, try **frappé** (with ice).

Shopping

For holidaymakers used to the 'Come to my shop, just one moment, please, where are you from?' style, which accompanies many popular holiday spots, shopping Corfu style is an absolute pleasure. Most shop owners are friendly without being pushy and quite happy for you to browse in peace, but it's still worth bartering for something expensive.

CERAMICS

Ceramics are available in a wide range of shapes and finishes. Many designs are copies of museum pieces and ancient Greek pottery. Brightly coloured fruit bowls, platters and mugs are also popular.

FOOD & DRINK

Attractive herb-and-spice sets, with small bottles of olive oil or miniatures of ouzo, make good presents. Large pots of honey, with pistachios or walnuts, or the delicious pistachio cream are inexpensive alternatives. Metaxa brandy is very good, especially the five- and seven-star, and much cheaper than at home, and all supermarkets sell *ouzo*.

⬥ *Afternoon sunlight illuminates the arcade below Corfu Town's Liston building*

JEWELLERY

From simple beaded chokers to silver bangles and gold necklaces, there's something to suit every taste. Gold is particularly good value as the purity tends to be higher than at home – at least 14 carat, and often 18. Traditional designs include the dolphin (often seen in the waters around Corfu), and the dying Achilles statue from the Achilleion Palace.

LACE & EMBROIDERY

Embroidered cotton and lacework is of high quality in Corfu, particularly around Kassiopi where you can see old women clad in black working their threads with nimble fingers. Look out for exquisite cotton table-cloths, crocheted tops, lace table-mats and coasters at reasonable prices.

LEATHER

Fluorescent orange suede, chic leather business bags, rough-and-ready holdalls – Corfu's the place to buy a handbag for every outfit. The leather is good quality but beware – items bearing designer names are usually fake; inspect the stitching before you buy. Decent, inexpensive buys include belts, leather slippers and gloves.

OLIVE WOOD

Wonderfully smooth, olive wood souvenirs range from enormous fruit bowls and pestle-and-mortar sets to more modest hairslides and carved animals. Original designs are most likely to be found in small family-run shops with an adjacent workshop, but the labour-intensive process of smoothing by hand is reflected in high-ish prices.

OLIVES

Olive wood is so plentiful because, under Venetian rule, farmers were paid 100 pieces of silver for every 100 olive trees they planted. There are over 3 million of these silver-green trees on Corfu today.

Children

If you're sightseeing in Corfu Town and the children are getting tired, revive them with a dip in the sea at **Mon Repos beach** (the far end of Garitsa Bay) or – not as clean but more central – **Alekos beach** (down a slope on the point before St Michael and St George's Palace).

WATERSPORTS

Aqualand (see page 40) is Corfu's best waterpark, situated inland between Ermones and Aghios Ioannis. Near Acharavi, you'll find **Hydropolis** (see page 63), a smaller waterpark near Acharavi is no less fun. Other water parks and slides can be found in Moraitika, Sidari and Aghios Ioannis (near Benitses). Older children that can swim well are welcome to participate in scuba diving; let them discover life beneath the waves on a short try dive excursion.

Older children that can swim well are welcome to participate in scuba diving; let them discover life beneath the waves on a short try dive excursion.

GO GREEK

Look out for restaurants advertising Greek dancing displays. Children are frequently invited to join in and may find themselves being balanced on the top of a table held by someone's teeth! They particularly relish plate-smashing sessions. Many hotels and bars also offer specific children's entertainment.

SIESTA

It's a good idea to encourage young children to have a siesta in the afternoon, not only to avoid the sun during the hottest hours of the day, but also because dance displays and entertainment typically start around 21.30.

The **Messonghi Beach Hotel** has a team of entertainers with a whole repertoire of songs and games to keep children on their toes (ⓐ Between Moraitika and Messonghi ① 26610 83000). A trip to the Greek evenings at **Korakiana** and **Kynopiastes** is fun for all ages (page 109).

🔺 *Water parks are great fun for children*

Sports & activities

After you've read a few books, supped a few beers and stopped waking up thinking you're late for work, you might fancy stretching your legs to see some of the glorious scenery Corfu has to offer. A gentle walk, a competitive game of golf or a rollercoaster bicycle ride through the hills – whatever – it's yours for the taking.

CYCLING

Cycling is an inexpensive way to explore the island. Hiring a mountain bike for the day is easy and cheap. Guided tours, which explore rural Corfu at a leisurely pace, are run by **The Corfu Mountainbike Shop** in Dassia (page 79) and **Mountain Mania** (ⓐ Main street, Sidari ⓘ 26630 95016).

GOLF

Corfu's 18-hole golf course nestles in the lush green surroundings of the Ropa Valley, 14 km (22 miles) west of Corfu Town. It's set against a backdrop of thickly wooded hills with a fair sprinkling of lakes, streams

⬤ There are many watersports on offer on Corfu

and tree-lined fairways to provide challenges for experienced golfers. Beginners can take their first swings amidst the spectacular scenery – half an hour's individual tuition is reasonably priced and there are discounts for groups.

HORSE RIDING

Sit back and enjoy the countryside and let the horse take the strain. A variety of excursions on horseback for all levels of experience are available from Sidari (see page 56, the **Yellow Boat Company**), and Ipsos (see page 75, **The Rider's Club**).

WALKING

Even the liveliest resorts are within just a few kilometres (a couple of miles) of peaceful countryside. Olive groves, lemon orchards, and paths dotted with an abundance of wild flowers await the visitor who ventures off the beaten track. Villages such as Spartilas, Strinilas, Episkepsi and Nimfes on the slopes of Mount Pantokrator offer glimpses of traditional Corfiot life, as does Ano Pavliana and the area around Aghios Mattheos.

Keen walkers should invest in a book called *The Corfu Trail* by Hilary Whitton-Paipeti, which contains information about the long-distance footpath which the author created, running from the southernmost to the northernmost point of the island.

WATERSPORTS

Whichever beach you choose, you'll be inundated with opportunities to test your skill – and sometimes your nerve – in the water. Activities vary from the fairly sedate, such as canoes and pedalos, to the more dynamic water-skiing, windsurfing and parascending. You can invest in a course of ten windsurfing lessons or a ten-hour sailing course. Diving is offered in various resorts around the island. Those offering internationally recognised PADI, CMAS or BSAC qualifications are a good starting point. Please note that you should allow at least 24 hours to elapse after your dive before flying.

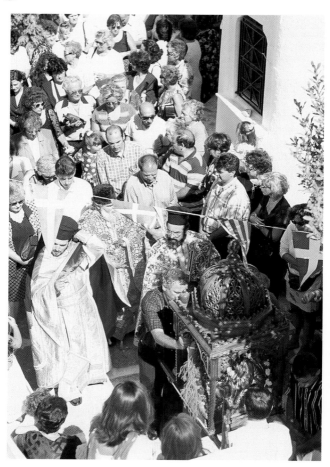

⬥ *Festival of the Assumption*

Festivals & events

GREEK NIGHTS

Dance and music are an integral part of Greek culture. Some restaurants have special Greek nights when you pay for a set menu dinner and show. Others offer dancing displays and entertainment at no extra charge.

Performed well, the various dances – *sirtaki* (better known as *Zorba the Greek*), *hasapiko* and *tsifteteli* (belly-dancing) – are spectacular finger-snapping, hand-clapping fun and holidaymakers will usually have a chance to learn a step or two.

Korakiana and **Kynopiastes** are the main dance venues in Corfu offering a thoroughly entertaining evening of traditional and modern Greek dance, belly-dancing, acrobatics, live singers, guitarists and *bouzouki* music (the *bouzouki* being a cross between a guitar and a banjo). The evening includes dinner and wine and can be booked from any resort on the island.

If you're in Corfu late in the year, 28 October is Ochi Day – an unashamedly patriotic national holiday with processions and dancing to commemorate the Greek Prime Minister's reply to Mussolini's call for Greek surrender in 1940 – No! (*Ochi!*).

ORTHODOX EASTER

Easter is the most important date in the Greek Orthodox calendar and can fall up to three weeks either side of the British Easter. Corfu Town is the place to be on Easter Saturday morning when you can see people throwing pots and crockery from their balconies (symbolising a fresh start to the year).

In the evening, after mass, there is a spectacular fireworks display before everyone goes home to eat a special lamb and vegetable soup called *mayeritsa*.

SAINTS' DAYS

Everyone in the Greek Orthodox church is named after a saint, and they celebrate their saint's feast day rather than their birthday. Throughout the year every village celebrates its church's name day. Many of these fall in the summer, so look out for the festivals, dancing and drinking which accompany them, but remember that much of the partying takes place on the evening before the actual day.

Some common saints' days to watch out for are 23 April, **St George's Day**, 29 June, **St Peter and St Paul's Day** and 17 July, **St Marina's Day**, which is widely celebrated in rural villages as she is the protector of crops. The **Assumption of the Virgin Mary**, on 15 August, is the most important day after Easter – it is a national holiday, when all the shops are closed.

The pretty **Barcarola** festival takes place in Garitsa Bay on 10 August. The street lamps are switched off, and floats decorated with fairy lights and candles illuminate the sea. Greek musicians and local dance schools performing in the streets add to the carnival atmosphere.

The most important church on the island is Saint Spiridon's in Corfu Town where the body of Saint Spiridon, the patron saint of Corfu, is placed in a silver-plated reliquary. His body, which some believe to have remained miraculously intact, was brought to Corfu from Constantinople in 1453. Local myth says that Saint Spiridon leaves the church and walks through the narrow streets of town every night – so your holy encounter may not have been an *ouzo*-induced vision after all!

▶ *Watching the world go by*

PRACTICAL INFORMATION
Tips & advice

Accommodation

Corfu has thousands of hotels, offering accommodation in all price ranges. Many hotels are only open between May and October, with July and August being the busiest months.

Hotel rates (double room rate with breakfast in high season):
£ = below €75 **££** = €75–150 **£££** = over €150

AGHIOS GEORGIOS (NW)
Blue Heaven £–££ Accommodation fitting with the quiet atmosphere in the resort, Blue heaven has pleasant studios and an apartment right on the seafront in the middle of the resort. ⓐ Seafront ⓣ 26630 96220 ⓦ www.corfublueheaven.com

AGHIOS GEORGIOS (SW)
Blue Sea £–££ Set back from the main road, and a short walk from the beach, this family-run hotel comes with a large barside pool and an excellent restaurant. ⓐ Main road ⓣ 26620 52624 ⓦ www.bluesea-hotel.com

Sea Breeze £–££ Set in the middle of the beautiful bay, this family-orientated beachside hotel has a pool, restaurant and comfy rooms. ⓐ Aghios Gordios beach ⓣ 26610 53214 ⓦ www.seabreezecorfu.gr

CORFU TOWN
Arcadion ££ An exclusive yet affordable hotel in the heart of the old Venetian part of town, overlooking the square and Old Fortress. ⓐ 2 Vlasopoulou Street ⓣ 26610 30104 ⓦ www.arcadionhotel.com

GLYFADA
Louis Grand ££–£££ Glyfada's main all-inclusive hotel is situated at the end of the beach, with decent rooms all sporting a balcony or terrace, and a nice pool area. Remember to eat out a few times to help the local tavernas! ⓐ Glyfada beach ⓣ 26610 94140 ⓦ www.louishotels.com

GOUVIA

Molfetta Beach Hotel ££ A nicely designed resort hotel set along the beach, just a short walk away from the bustle of the main street. Rooms are comfortable with own balconies, and there's a great restaurant on site. ⓐ Gouvia seafront ⓣ 22610 91915 ⓦ www.molfettabeach.com

IPSOS

Sunrise £–££ Modern rooms and studios on a quiet stretch of the Ipsos seafront. There's a good pool at the back of the complex, and a restaurant along the street. ⓐ Main road ⓣ 26610 93414 ⓦ www.sunrise-corfu.com

MORAITIKA

Messonghi Beach Hotel ££ Great for both parents and children; this large complex has an unrivalled activities programme, well-tended grounds, a good pool and a safe beach right on the doorstep. ⓐ Moraitika beach ⓣ 26610 83000 ⓦ www.messonghibeach.gr

PALEOKASTRITSA

Apollon £–££ A modern hotel in the heart of Paleokastritsa, within walking distance of several beaches. Rooms have ISDN connections and there's a good bar and restaurant on site. ⓐ Main road ⓣ 26630 41211 ⓦ www.corfu-apollon-hotel.com

SIDARI

Akti Aphrodite £ The small Akti Aphrodite has efficient, small rooms overlooking the pool and beach. There's a lively bar too. ⓐ Sidari beachfront ⓣ 26630 95247 ⓦ www.aktiaphrodite.com

Preparing to go

GETTING THERE

The cheapest way to get to Corfu is to book a package holiday with one of the leading tour operators, often offering flight-only deals or combined flight-and-accommodation packages at prices that are hard to beat. The flight time from London is 3–4 hours. There are numerous charter airline companies offering flights to Greece during the summer months, although if you travel out of season, you may have to use a scheduled flight with British Airways (📞 0870 850 9 850 🌐 www.ba.com) or Olympic Airlines (📞 0870 60 60 460 🌐 www.olympicairlines.com) to Athens and a connecting flight with Olympic Airlines or Aegean Airlines (🌐 www.aegeanair.com) to Corfu. You can also choose to use one of many budget airlines flying from Western Europe to Corfu; see 🌐 www.whichbudget.com for a complete overview of connections. If you can be flexible about when you visit, you can pick up relatively inexpensive special deals. As a rule, the further in advance you buy your ticket, the cheaper it usually is – but you can also get good last-minute deals from online travel agents via the internet.

Many people are aware that air travel emits CO_2, which contributes to climate change. You may be interested in the possibility of lessening the environmental impact of your flight through the charity Climate Care, which offsets your CO_2 by funding environmental projects around the world. Visit 🌐 www.climatecare.org

TOURISM AUTHORITY

In the UK, the **Greek National Tourist Office** (🅰 4 Conduit Street, London W1S 2DJ 📞 020 7495 9300 ✉ info@gnto.co.uk 🌐 www.gnto.co.uk) can provide general information about visiting Greece, and has useful brochures and maps that you can download online or order. The official **Rhodes Town website** has a wealth of historical information and tips. Visit 🌐 www.rhodes.gr

BEFORE YOU LEAVE

It is not necessary to have inoculations to travel in Europe, but you should make sure you and your family are up to date with the basics, such as tetanus. It is a good idea to pack a small first-aid kit to carry with you containing plasters, antiseptic cream, travel sickness pills, insect repellent and/or bite-relief cream, antihistamine tablets, upset stomach remedies and painkillers. Suntan lotion and after-sun cream are more expensive in Greece than in the UK so it is worth taking some. Take your prescription medicines along as you may find it impossible to obtain the same medicines in Greece.

Although Greece is a very safe country when it comes to petty crime and has a good healthcare system, it's a good idea to purchase travel insurance before you go. Check the policy carefully regarding medical coverage, dental treatment, loss of baggage, flight cancellations, repatriation, etc., and whether activities like scuba diving, horse riding and watersports need extra coverage. Keep all medical receipts for claim purposes; if your possessions are stolen, you'll also need to file a police report. UK visitors carrying a European Health Insurance Card (EHIC) get reduced-cost and sometimes free state-provided medical treatment in Greece and most other European countries. The free card can be ordered via the Department of Health (📞 0845 606 2030 🌐 www.ehic.org.uk).

ENTRY FORMALITIES

All EU and other citizens from all Western countries only need a passport to enter Greece. Visas are only required by certain nationalities; details can be found on the **Greek Foreign Ministry** website 🌐 www.mfa.gr. All children, including newborn babies, need their own passports unless they are already included on the passport of the person they are travelling with. For the latest information on passports, contact the Identity & Passport Service (📞 0870 521 0410 🌐 www.passport.gov.uk). Check the details of your travel tickets well before your departure, ensuring that the timings and dates are correct. If you plan to rent a car in Greece, be sure to have your driving licence (and that of any other driver) with you.

MONEY

Like many EU countries, Greece uses the euro. Euro (€) note denominations are 500, 200, 100, 50, 20, 10 and 5. Coins are 1 and 2 euros and 1, 2, 5, 10, 20 and 50 centimos (also called lepta). At time of research the exchange rate was £0.68 to the euro. The best way to get euros on Corfu is by using your debit bank card in an ATM, which can be found in all towns, in most resorts and at the airport and harbour. Make sure you know your PIN and check with your bank to see if there are any charges for using your card abroad; Nationwide is the only UK bank offering free ATM transactions abroad. Credit cards are increasingly accepted in Greek resort hotels and restaurants, but less so in shops and supermarkets. Check the validity date and credit limit of your cards before you go. You can purchase cash euros before leaving the UK, but keep in mind that changing cash locally at a bank or exchange office will be much better value. Euro-denomination traveller's cheques, which can be purchased at UK exchange offices and banks, are a safe way to carry money as you'll be refunded if the cheques are lost or stolen, but they're used less and less in Europe and can be a hassle to change. If you're going on a day trip to Albania you can easily exchange euros, British pounds or US dollars for Albanian lek on arrival, or use an ATM.

CLIMATE

The weather on Corfu is generally good. There is always the possibility of a windy spell or a short burst of rain, but this won't last more than a day or two. July and August are the hottest months, with maximum daytime temperatures around 34°C (93°F) but sometimes going over 40°C (104°F), and it's best to stay out of the sun from 11.00 to 15.00. June and September are slightly cooler, with daytime temperatures rarely exceeding 30°C (86°F). During late-May and early-October, it's still just about possible to swim, but the weather can be unpredictable, with temperatures rarely exceeding 25°C (77°F). In high season, pack some light cotton clothes so you can cover up when you've had enough sun. Even during summer, temperatures can drop rapidly at night, so you should also bring at least one light jumper or jacket.

BAGGAGE ALLOWANCE

Baggage allowances vary according to the airline, destination and the class of travel, but 20 kg (44 lb) per person is the norm for luggage that is carried in the hold; check your ticket to see if the weight limit is mentioned there. Large items – surfboards, golf-clubs, collapsible wheelchairs and pushchairs – are usually charged as extras, and it is a good idea to let the airline know in advance if you want to bring these. You are allowed only one item of hand baggage measuring 55 by 40 by 20 cm (22 by 16 by 8 in) plus any airport purchases, umbrella, handbag, coat, camera, etc. Note that security measures at both UK and Greek airports prohibit you from taking any sharp objects or any liquids and gels in your hand baggage, except liquids necessary for the flight and packed in containers no larger than 100 ml (3½ oz) inside resealable plastic bags. Read more about the security rules on your departure airport website.

◆ Take a day trip to Albania on a hydrofoil with Ionian Cruises

During your stay

AIRPORTS

Corfu airport is small, disorganised, chaotic and often crowded – make sure you arrive well before departure time and bring plenty of patience, drinks and snacks in case you have to wait outside for a long time. It's so close to Corfu Town that you can walk from the terminal to the city centre in about half an hour, but taxis are at hand, many rental car agencies have offices at the airports, and regular buses to and from the south of the island stop along the main road, 300 m (330 yds) from the terminal building. Note that it's often cheaper to arrange car hire in advance, and that in high season cars can be difficult to come by without advance booking.

COMMUNICATIONS

The Greek national phone company, **OTE**, has public phones in all towns, villages and resorts which accept OTE phone cards and have English-language instructions. Some resorts have private coin-operated phone booths but these are usually very bad value. You can also make calls from many kiosks or from a kafenion in smaller villages; they have a metering system and you will be told how much your call costs at the end. Using a €5 prepaid calling card (available at any kiosk) is the cheapest way to phone abroad. These can be used from any OTE public phone or hotel phone.

Many tourists bring their mobile phones along and use roaming to phone home. Check the charges carefully as this can be a very expensive way to phone home. If you're planning to phone often and want to be reached as well, consider buying a local Cosmote or Vodafone SIM card (available from many kiosks and mobile phone shops for a few euros) so you have a local number incurring lower costs.

Post

Most post offices are open 08.00–14.30 Mon–Fri, the main one in Corfu Town 07.30–20.00 Mon–Fri and Sat mornings in high season. Post boxes are bright yellow with a blue logo on; at major post offices you will find two slots – *esoterik* for local mail and *exoterik* for overseas. Outside the main towns they are not always emptied every day. Postcards can take up to two weeks to get to Britain, letters three or four days; if you want your postcards to arrive back home before you do then put them in an envelope. Sending a postcard or letter abroad costs €0.62.

CUSTOMS

Greeks are usually very friendly to strangers, and you are bound to experience traditional hospitality in one way or another during your stay. Greeks rarely begin their evening meal earlier than 21.00, and usually take the whole family along, babies too. Children are generally allowed to wander around restaurants at will, even late at night.

TELEPHONING TO AND IN GREECE

All telephone numbers in Greece, whether landline or mobile phones, consist of ten digits, and there are no additional city codes. To make a call within Greece, simply dial these ten digits. To call to Greece from abroad or from your mobile phone while in the country, dial the international access code, usually 00, followed by Greece's country code +30 and the ten-digit local number.

TELEPHONING ABROAD

To call abroad from Greece, dial 00 followed by the country code followed by the city code (minus the initial 0) and the subscriber's number.

44 for the UK
353 for Ireland
1 for the US and Canada
61 for Australia
64 for New Zealand
27 for South Africa

DRESS CODES

If you are visiting churches or monasteries you will not be allowed in wearing shorts or beach clothes; it is best to wear long trousers or a skirt and take a shirt or wrap to cover your shoulders. Some churches provide clothing for visitors to wear. Topless sunbathing is officially forbidden but still common in some beach resorts; judge the situation before stripping and causing upset.

ELECTRICITY

Greece has 220 V (50 Hertz) electrical outlets. You will need an adaptor plug for any electrical equipment you bring with you and these can be purchased at the local supermarkets or in the UK before you depart. At times in high season there may be power cuts lasting at most two hours, but usually much less. It is important to realise that electricity is expensive in Greece, so be considerate and do not leave lights and air-conditioning on in your room when you go out.

GETTING AROUND

Driving conditions

Remember that in Greece you drive on the right. Always carry your driving licence, passport and any other relevant documents with you when driving, and ask for a map when renting the car. The road quality on Corfu is generally quite good, with only a few smaller roads and unsurfaced tracks requiring you to slow down to protect your wheel

Emergency numbers in Corfu are as follows:
Police (general) 112
Tourist police ⓐ 4 Samartzi, Corfu Town ⓣ 22610 30265
Fire 112
Ambulance 112

For medical treatment:
Corfu Town Hospital ⓣ 22610 30033

rims. The main roads leading to and from Corfu Town get congested in high season, and it's a good idea to avoid the road running past the airport towards Perama, as it is closed down for a few minutes each time a plane takes off. In high season beware slow drivers, holidaymakers on quad motorbikes, farmers watering their olives and traffic jams. Beware of illegal parking in Corfu Town, as the police are quick to hand out fines. Forget about parking in the centre on weekdays, it's notoriously difficult to find a spot. If you are stopped by the police for a motoring offence you are expected to pay your fine on the spot (make sure you get a receipt if you do). If you do not pay, the police will remove the licence plates from your car, which you will then have to reclaim from the police station on payment of the fine. If anything like this happens you should contact your hire company immediately.

Car hire and driving

Drivers need to be over 21 years old (25 in some cases) and have a valid driving licence. Car hire is available at most resorts and costs €30–60 per day for a small car, depending on season and length of rental. Local rental companies in the beach resorts often have lower prices than the international companies in the main towns. Most rental cars are new and zippy small cars, and air-conditioning is quite common. Open-top 4WDs are popular but much pricier. Insurance is included in your car rental, but is sometimes not valid if you use non-asphalted roads; and check that it includes damage to the wheels, tyres and roof.

Public transport

Bus transport on Corfu is quite good, with regular departures for most towns and resorts. Blue city buses serve the local area around Corfu Town (Kontokali, Perama, Kanoni, etc.) and depart from Platia Saroko. Green air-conditioned buses run by **KTEL** (information ☎ 26610 39862) link Corfu Town to towns and resorts across the island; the bus station is on Avramiou Street near the New Fortress. Timetables can be found at the tourist offices and at the bus station, where you can also buy tickets in advance. When getting on in villages and resorts you usually pay the conductor after getting seated. Note that services on Sunday are very limited or non-existent.

Taxis

Taxis can be found at arrival points, major hotels and driving around the larger resorts. They're comparatively inexpensive to use, and prices for longer distances are usually fixed. There's a surcharge after midnight. Any hotel or restaurant will call a taxi for you on request.

HEALTH, SAFETY & CRIME

Healthcare

There are a number of private medical clinics offering a 24-hour service and with English-speaking doctors. Details are available at local *Pharmakia* (pharmacies). Pharmacies often have English-speaking staff and are very helpful for minor complaints and illnesses. They operate a rota system for opening outside normal shop hours (especially at the weekend) and information about the duty chemist is displayed in each shop. Generally both over-the-counter and prescription drugs purchased at pharmacies will be cheaper than in England. However, some, such as antibiotics, can be expensive. Homeopathic and herbal treatments and remedies are very popular in Greece and widely available. Personal hygiene goods are found in supermarkets.

Water

Tap water is safe enough, but bottled water is cheap, widely available, and tastes much better.

Safety & crime

Compared to most western European countries, Greece is a very safe place, with hardly any petty or violent crime – in fact, it's mainly other tourists, and not Greeks, that you have to be wary of! A forgotten camera or wallet will most likely still be on the restaurant table when you return for it, and public drunkenness or violence is quite rare. Still, avoid temptation by leaving all valuables and documents in the hotel safe and carrying only what you need. Be wary for bag snatchers in busy resorts and towns, and leave your car empty when you park it. The police keep a low profile but invariably turn up when needed at motor accidents and crime scenes, and to deal with illegally parked cars. There are also tourist police, who speak several languages and are trained to help with problems faced by tourists.

MEDIA

It's easy to stay in touch with home, as many resorts sell English newspapers, usually only a day or two out of date. *The Corfiot* is a monthly magazine written by British expats on Corfu, and can be ordered via Ⓦ www.thecorfiotmagazine.com. Most hotels with televisions and English bars have satellite TV for a dose of sports and news. The online English edition of Greece's *Kathimerini* newspaper is a good source of national news (Ⓦ www.ekathimerini.com). There's also a section detailing festivals around Greece.

OPENING HOURS

Shops traditionally open from 08.00–14.30 Mon & Wed, 08.00–14.00 & 17.00–20.00 Tues, Thur, Fri and 08.00–13.00 Sat. Tourist resorts are a case apart and most shops open all day, usually from early morning until 23.00. Sunday is a general closing day, but shops serving tourism mostly remain open.

Banks are open 08.00–14.00 Mon–Thur and 08.00– 13.30 Fri. A few branches in the island capitals are also open from 09.00–13.00 Sat.

Restaurants are generally often open 09.00–23.00. Breakfast ends around 10.00, lunch is usually between 13.30–15.30 and dinner starts late for Greeks – 20.00 is on the early side.

Churches are almost always open for visiting, but in villages you often have to find the lady in black who looks after the key.

RELIGION

Greece is dominated by the Greek Orthodox Church with a faith that has strong historical roots in the local community. Saints' days and name days are very important days to celebrate. Weddings, baptisms and funerals are serious and lengthy occasions. Be respectful and cover up before you enter a church or chapel.

TIME DIFFERENCES

Greece is in the Eastern European time zone, 2 hours ahead of the UK, 5 hours ahead of EST and 4 hours ahead of CST. Clocks go forward 1 hour on the last Sunday in March and back 1 hour on the last Sunday in October.

TIPPING

In restaurants a service or cover charge is often included in your bill. However, if the service warrants it you can leave a small tip to the waiters or bar staff; 5–10% is about right. Taxi drivers don't expect tips but if you are happy with the service, give a tip. If you are shown around a church by the 'keyholder' or priest, a tip is also welcome, but this should always be left in the donations box rather than offered directly to the guide.

TOILETS

Public toilets are found in bus stations and main squares. Smarter facilities are found in bars, but you should buy a drink or ask nicely if you want to use them. Toilets are generally very clean, but you must observe the practice throughout Greece and not flush away used toilet paper. Do as the Greeks do and put it in a bin (provided in each cubicle) next to the toilet. Remember this, or you risk blocking the pipes!

TRAVELLERS WITH DISABILITIES

Greece is slowly catching up with the rest of the EU when it comes to facilities for the disabled. Many ramps have now been built onto beaches and in hotel and restaurant entrances, and some of the local buses have disabled access, but this is normally restricted to people on foot, not in wheelchairs. The island towns and resorts are mainly flat and easy to get around. Some hotels have facilities for disabled people, but there are still very few taxis or buses that can cope with a motorised wheelchair.

A

accommodation 112–13
Acharavi 63–5
Achilleion Palace 10, 36, 86–7
Afionas 47
Aghios Georgios (north-west) 11, 47–8, 112
Aghios Georgios (south-west) 10, 30–2, 112
Aghios Gordios 10, 33–5, 112
Aghios Ioannis (St John's) 20
Aghios Markos 74
Aghios Stefanos 11, 51–3
Agni 68–9
air travel 114, 118
Albania 8, 11, 88–9, 116
Almyros 60
Analipsis 22
Angelokastro 43
Aqualand 40–1
Argirades 30
Arillas 49–50, 51
ATMs 116

B

baggage allowances 117
banks 123
Barbati 72–3, 74
beaches 9, 104
    naturist beaches 36, 60
    see also individual locations
Benitses 20–1
birdwatching 30–1
Blue Eye Caves 43
boat trips 17, 24, 28, 30, 37, 43, 51, 66, 72, 74, 79, 89, 94
Boukari 24
bowling 55
bungee jumping 27
buses 121–2
Butrint 11, 88–9

C

Cape Asprokavos 27–8
car hire 115, 121

casino 23

children 104, 119
Cliffs of Aerostato 33
climate 116
consulate 120
Corfu Town 9, 10, 14–19, 112
credit cards 116
crime 122–3
customs, local 119
cycling 55–6, 79, 106

D

Dassia 79–80
Diapontia islands 51
disabilities, travellers with 124
dress codes 120
drinking water 122
driving 115, 120–1

E

eating out 96–101, 123
    see also individual locations
electricity 120
emergencies 120
entertainment see individual locations
Ermones 39–41

F

festivals and events 108–10
food and drink 96–101, 102

G

Glyfada 36–8, 113
go-karting 27, 56, 75
golf 39–40, 106–7
Gouvia 81–4, 113

H

health 115, 122
horse carriage rides 56
horse riding 40, 56, 60, 75, 107
Hydropolis 63

I

inoculations 115
insurance 115
Ipsos 74–8, 113

K

kafeneion (café) 101
Kalami 68–9
Kanoni peninsula 22
Kassiopi 66–7
Kavos 11, 27–9
Kontokali 81–4

L

Lake Korission 30
Lakones 44–5
language 100–1
Liapades 45

M

Makrades 45
medical treatment 115, 120, 122
menu decoder 100–1
Messonghi 24–6
money 116
Moraitika 24–6, 113
Mount Pantokrator 11, 63, 75
Mouse Island 22
Myrtiotissa 36

N

newspapers 123
Nissaki 70–1
Nymphes 60

O

Old Perithia 63
opening hours 123

P

paintballing 79
Paleokastritsa 9, 11, 42–6, 113
parasailing 51
Parga 90–2
passports and visas 115

Paxos 93–4
Pelekas 36–8
Perama 20–3
pharmacies 122
Platanos 60
police 120, 123
Pontikonisi 22
postal services 118–19

R

religion 123–4
Roda 60–2

S

St Peter's 27
scuba diving 11, 24, 28, 31, 34, 40, 44, 47, 75, 107
Sfakera 60
shopping 102–3, 123
    see also individual locations
Sidari 54–9, 113
Sinarades 33–4
sports and activities 106–7
Sunset Beach 55

T

taxis 122
telephones 118, 119
television 123
tennis 24, 51
Theotokos Monastery 45
time differences 124
tipping 124
toilets 124
tourist information 114
traveller's cheques 116

W

walking 27–8, 47, 51, 52, 60, 107
water parks 40–1, 63, 104
watersports 24, 27, 28, 31, 34, 36, 47, 49, 56–7, 68, 72, 107
windsurfing 47

Y

Yialiskari Bay 68

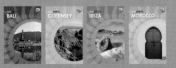

ACKNOWLEDGEMENTS

The publishers would like to thank all the photographers, picture libraries and organisations for the loan of the photographs reproduced in this book, to whom copyright in the photograph belongs:
Iain Frazer/BigStockPhoto page 10; Pictures Colour Library pages 1, 17, 29, 69, 97, 98, 105, 108, 117; Thomas Schoch/Wikimedia Commons pages 87, 111; Jennifer Slot/Flickr.com pages 44, 56; Spectrum Colour Library page 71, 83; Jeroen van Marle pages 37, 39; World Pictures/Photoshot pages 8, 89; all the rest Thomas Cook Tour Operations Ltd.

Project editor: Alison Coupe
Layout: Donna Pedley
Proofreader: Soo Hamilton
Indexer: Marie Lorimer

Send your thoughts to
books@thomascook.com

- Found a beach bar, peaceful stretch of sand or must-see sight that we don't feature?

- Like to tip us off about any information that needs a little updating?

- Want to tell us what you love about this handy, little guidebook and more importantly how we can make it even handier?

Then here's your chance to tell all! Send us ideas, discoveries and recommendations today and then look out for your valuable input in the next edition of this title.

Send an email to the above address or write to:
HotSpots Series Editor, Thomas Cook Publishing, PO Box 227, Unit 9, Coningsby Road, Peterborough PE3 8SB, UK.